Shortcuts to Success

Study and Exam Skills for Leaving Certificate

Irene Togher

Gill & Macmillan

Gill & Macmillan Ltd
Hume Avenue
Park West
Dublin 12
with associated companies throughout the world
www.gillmacmillan.ie

© Irene Togher, 2007
Artwork by Kate Shannon

978 0 7171 4169 2

Print origination in Ireland by Carole Lynch

The paper used in this book is made from the wood pulp of managed forests. For every tree felled, at least one tree is planted, thereby renewing natural resources.

Contents

As parents, you want to help and support your children through study and exams. This section shows you how you can support your child in a practical way during the school year. It outlines how you can help motivate your child; how you can keep your children healthy while they are studying; how you can help them in the run-up to the exams and what to do if you think your child could be working harder.

This section shows you how to get organised so that you can study effectively. It outlines how you can begin by maintaining good physical and mental health throughout the school year and during exams. You will also learn how to form good study habits, motivate yourself and manage your time.

Doing well in exams and study means taking it all in – absorbing and retaining information. This section guides you through the different skills you need to do this – reading to learn and reading to answer questions; listening, note taking and using memory tricks to increase your ability to remember facts.

Dedication

Every word of this book is dedicated to my beautiful, amazing mother, who has invested so much in my education.

Acknowledgements

I would like to thank the following teachers for their contributions to the exam guide appendices. You were all so generous with your time and expertise. I really appreciate it.

Padraig Browne: Physics
Mary Donnellan: Mathematics
Caroline Gough: Irish
Tony Magner: Geography
Mairead Mulvin: Business Studies
Sarah McNally: Biology and Chemistry (and for the weather tip!)
Owen Swaine: History
Mary Sheridan: French (and for the advice on the oral exams chapter)
Claire Wynne: Home Economics

Introduction

If we wanted to do any job like carpentry, teaching, bricklaying or medical research we would have to learn the skills needed to complete the various tasks involved. Yet we all tend to launch into learning and study without ever considering that there are skills involved that we should master first.

This book aims to help you equip yourself with the skills you'll need in your school career to learn, study and do exams.

Learning can be a frustrating business. Often, we feel dejected because we have too many tasks and not enough time. We sometimes don't know where to start and it feels overwhelming. And then when we finally do get down to doing some learning, the next day we've forgotten almost it all and we start to think, why bother?

Couple this with some depressing statistics about not being able to concentrate for more than 45 minutes at a time and losing 80% of what we learn within eight days and we're almost ready to throw in the towel.

The purpose of this book though is to help you beat these odds. With some careful strategies and some useful techniques, you'll learn the skills necessary for study and exam success.

It's not essential that you read this book from front cover to back cover in perfect order. Feel free to dip in and out as you need advice. Each section is self-contained and can be read in isolation.

Section 1 is for parents. This section offers parents some advice on helping and supporting their children through school and exams.

The rest of the book begins with the basic foundation skills that will stand to your benefit in all your learning. The first section shows you how to prepare for and organise your study. Chapter 1 explores ways you can maintain your overall physical and mental health throughout the school year and during exams. It discusses diet, exercise and even includes exercises that will teach you how to relax if you find yourself getting stressed. It also shows you how to organise timetables, organise a study space and generally establish good study habits throughout the year.

Section 2 shows you how you can 'take it all in'. Here, you will learn how to master reading, listening, and note-taking skills. You will also, I hope, enjoy learning about different memory tricks that you can use for retaining information that you are learning both in class and at home.

In Section 4, you will learn how to express yourself clearly and logically in writing. I outline key grammar, spelling and punctuation rules and highlight the importance of good structure when it comes to writing sentences and paragraphs. You will find this a very useful reference tool throughout your studies.

Finally, you'll learn the strategies needed for preparing for and sitting successful exams – written, oral and aural.

Even though you'll have all the skills necessary for study and exams when you finish this book, you may still find work difficult. If this is the case, never be afraid to ask for help. Teachers are there to support and guide you. They want you to do well. Ask for help and you'll get it.

Good luck in your learning endeavours.

Section 1

Guide for Parents

It is every parent's aim to provide the best possible life for his or her children. When it comes to education, you want the best for them. When it comes to exams, you want to provide as much support as you can. However, you may sometimes feel fairly powerless. Rather than actually going in and sitting the exam for your daughter or son, you might feel that there is very little you can do to help her or him along.

This isn't true though. The support and encouragement you give your teenage daughter or son can make all the difference in giving her or him the best opportunity possible to do well at study and exams. Think of yourself as the background crew in a film. You set the scene and provide the background support and environment where the actors can perform their best without worrying about the little details. Many students don't really know how to study and learn and this book aims to guide them through the best ways to organise their studies for maximum learning.

The fact that you have bought this book shows an interest in your child's school career that is admirable. You have already taken a step to supporting your child. The rest of the support you give throughout the year will help keep your child focused on study and learning as he or she goes through the school year, while your patience and encouragement at exam time can help ease the exam process to something a lot less stressful than it can sometimes be.

This section shows you:

- how you can support your child in a practical way during the school year
- how you can help motivate your child
- how to keep your child healthy while they are studying
- how to support your child before, during and after the exams.

During the school year

Throughout the school year, support and guide your student as much as you can. You can do this by making sure they attend school, providing a study-friendly environment, offering motivation, encouraging routine and keeping your child healthy.

School attendance

It is essential that your child attend school regularly. Try not to allow your daughter or son to miss days without good reason. If they do miss too many days, it can mean they fall back in work. Or if the teacher starts a new topic and the student misses the early explanations, it can sometimes be almost impossible to follow along later.

Stay informed

Stay informed about your child's progress in school. Attend the parent–teacher meetings and meet all your child's teachers. Ask for a progress report from each of them.

It's usually a good idea to bring a notepad and pen with you to the meeting, as it's easy to forget what teacher said what about which subject. Don't be embarrassed to ask questions and take notes.

If you can't make the meeting or you are particularly worried about your child at another time of the year, contact the school. Teachers are always willing to meet with a parent if you request an appointment beforehand. Try not to just turn up at the school expecting to meet a particular teacher though, as teachers can't leave classes unattended to chat in the hall and they may not have any relevant notes with them at that moment. It's better to arrange a time suitable for both of you.

If you're looking for a more general update on your child's progress you can request a report from the school, which all teachers will fill in and the school will send to you.

Create a study-friendly environment

It is essential that your student has a study-friendly environment. They will need a quiet place to work, so, if you can, set up a desk for them in a quiet room. Make sure too that the room is well lit and well ventilated.

Some students do homework in the kitchen or dining room but this is not generally a good idea. These are usually busy rooms, and too many distractions will block your child's ability to work. Your child's bedroom, a spare room or office are better options.

If possible, buy your student a study desk and comfortable office chair. Make sure they have all the supplies they need, like stationery, a reading lamp and folders.

While your child studies, TV, radio or video games are distractions, so it's worth checking that these have been turned off during the time when your child is working on homework and learning.

Encourage reading

I cannot overemphasise how important reading is for students. Access to a wide range of material like newspapers, novels, and magazines is vital. He or she will be exposed to a wide vocabulary, a wide range of writing styles and ideas and current topics in the news. All these are of huge benefit to a student, so do all you can to foster an atmosphere of reading at home. If you're not already a member, it's worth joining your local library so that your home has access to a wide range of up-to-date and free reading materials.

Decide levels

Make sure your child chooses what level (higher or ordinary) he or she wants to sit some time before the actual exam. It's usually best if this is done immediately after the Mock Exams. Work with your child and the teacher to make this decision.

Encourage your child to make the decision though and stick to it. Don't encourage last-minute panic-stricken changes. Often students will panic at the last minute and take a lower paper. Remind your child that if they have put in the work, they should do the level they have prepared for.

Offer motivation

The main ways to motivate your child to study is to help them set goals and targets, reward work well done, stay positive and establish routine.

Help set goals and targets

It is essential that your child has something to aim for when all this study is over and done with. Encourage them to set goals. **Goals** are the long-term aims that your child has – perhaps going to university or getting a good job after school. Talk to your child about their goals. Discuss fairly regularly that they still have this goal; encourage them to discuss it with the career guidance teacher; and be aware of the requirements for entry to college or the workplace.

Whose goals?

Make sure you listen to *their* goals. Quite often parents encourage their children to become perhaps a solicitor and can put a lot of pressure on the child to achieve this. What is important to ask is: is this your child's goal or is it a goal you would have for yourself if you were back in school? So make sure you listen to your child and encourage him or her to follow his or her own dream.

On a weekly basis though, your child will also need to break down the process it will take to reach this long-term goal into short-term **targets**. Encourage him or her to have a weekly 'to-do list' of study tasks for the week. This list should be kept realistic and specific. They will find out more about setting targets and organising to-do lists in Chapter 5.

Reward work done well

If your student achieves these weekly targets, it's a good idea to reward work done well. Most people like to work towards something positive, so offer rewards whenever you can to encourage your child to keep working hard.

You know yourself that a reward doesn't have to be expensive or even materialistic. It could be something like time to watch his or her favourite TV programme, which you taped during the week, time out with friends, space to play his or her loud music or just a picnic in the park – something that you think your child will enjoy and will take them out of the study room.

What is *very important* is to keep in mind that it is usually better to reward a strong work ethic throughout the year rather than just a good test mark. So, you need to encourage the work routine, not just concentrate on the grades. Emphasising the grades only adds pressure onto your child's shoulders.

Stay positive

It's vital to focus on positive achievements. When your child gets a class test back, congratulate them on any work that was done well. Even if he or she didn't get the hoped-for mark, try to find something positive to praise first and then encourage him or her to study even better the next time for a better grade. Praise before you criticise.

Help establish a routine

Study becomes a lot easier the more you do it, so it's important that your child maintains a routine of studying throughout the school year. Allow them to study at the same time and in the same place every evening. At this time, try not to disturb them and keep younger children away from them.

If this isn't possible at home, find out if there is a supervised study facility at school and encourage your child to take advantage of it.

Understand study patterns

Most people work in 45-minute slots and then take a break. So try to make sure that your child takes these regular breaks, as they help to re-establish concentration and prevent tiredness setting in too soon. However, these breaks should only be about 5-10 minutes, so keep an eye that they go back to work as soon as the 10 minutes is up.

The importance of balance

Part of any student's routine should be a good balance between work and leisure. Make sure that your child keeps up some other activities outside schoolwork like sport or music or whatever it is they *enjoy* doing for leisure.

Even if your child is not interested in sport, it's a good idea to encourage them to take up some physical activity – perhaps walking, aerobics, yoga, dance or cycling. Not only will it have beneficial results for your child's overall health, but it also helps overall mental health.

You can take a look at the student's guide to 'Getting Organised to Study: Guide for Students' below for more details in these areas.

Keep your child healthy

As you know, good health is vital for exam and study success. So, it's worth keeping an eye on your child's diet, exercise and rest in order to ensure they stay in good health throughout the year.

Diet

Healthy eating is essential for both a healthy body and a healthy brain. You can help by making sure that your child gets lots of fresh food like fruit, vegetables and high-protein meals with meat (especially lean chicken or beef), fish or pulses.

Breakfast is a particularly important meal, so encourage your child to eat breakfast every morning, with eggs, wholemeal bread, toast and fresh juice as some of the best options.

The best way to help your child in eating healthily is to *not* put temptation to eat junk food in their way. So try not to buy too many crisps, sweets, cakes or fizzy drinks. Try instead to always have a bowl of fruit in sight – include grapes, bananas, mandarins, perhaps a fresh pineapple as a treat. Many teenagers will eat fruit if they can see it. It's also a good idea to have nuts, yoghurts and plenty of fresh juices available for snacks.

Exercise

As well as a good diet, your child needs plenty of exercise. Encourage them to walk every day and don't allow them to give up sport in favour of study. The break from mental activity alone is essential for a balanced life, and exercise is good for overall health, stamina and concentration.

Sleep

Rest is another must-have. A good eight-hour's sleep every night is essential. Tiredness has all sorts of negative effects on your child in relation to motivation, mood, outlook, stamina and overall mental capacity.

For more detailed advice on these areas, take a look at Chapter 1, 'Keeping well'.

Space

While it is important that you are there to support your son or daughter in their study throughout the year, you must balance this with giving your child *space to work*. Try not to 'crowd' your child.

You know best if your child is the type of person who likes to talk about schoolwork or not. If they do, then encourage them to talk but, if not, then don't push it. If you push things too far, you'll probably find that your child will do even less work just to annoy you. Above all, avoid the awful trap of nagging. It will only cause a rift between you and your child.

Trust your student to do the work and to know what needs to be done. Give them all the support they need but then step back and give them the space to work.

What if your child is not working?

If you continue to feel though that your child is not doing the right work or enough of it, consult the teacher – he or she will know very well what progress your child is making. If the news is not encouraging, the worst thing you can do is come home and start shouting at your child. (Remember, teenagers tend to thrive on confrontation.)

Instead, ask the teacher for one or two positive factors you can focus on and talk about these with your child first. You can then move on to discuss areas for improvement with them. It's worth reassuring your son or daughter that you will help in any way you can. You must then leave the rest to your child.

Closer to the exams

As exam time approaches, students can get very nervous, anxious, panicky and moody, so be prepared. Try to avoid confrontations at this time. Just continue being in the background with healthy meals, encouragement and a positive attitude. Make yourself available to talk to your child if he or she needs you.

Again, you will know if your child likes to talk through things or not: if they do, then encourage this. Students love to hear about others people's experiences in exams and school, so share your own exam experiences with your child (the positive and funny ones preferably).

It is essential in the run-up to exams that your child sticks to the work routine that they have already established. This also means allowing time out for leisure and exercise. Some students will panic at this stage and try and cram as much study in as possible. However, this is generally not a good idea. While they can perhaps add a few more hours to their weekend schedule now, it is better to stick to the routine they have set up. The breaks now are even more important than ever, as stress levels at this time tend to be high.

Remind your child that their life will not end after the exam if they don't do as well as they hope. Give them some examples of people who have done well in life without perfect exam results.

Encourage them to do their best only and try not to put on any added pressure. Don't discuss points for college at this stage or high grades. If your child brings up this topic, encourage them to put it to the back of their mind for now.

If your child is particularly panicky, urge them to do some relaxation exercises (see Chapter 1, 'Keeping well') and to talk to school friends or their teacher.

The week before the exam

Find your child's official exam timetable. If this has been misplaced, don't panic. You can print one out from the internet from the Department of Education and Science (http//www.education.ie) or ask the school of another one. Pin this up in a prominent position in the house, like on the fridge or a notice board in the kitchen. Highlight your child's exams and check the days and times.

Work out how your child is going to get to and from the exams. Your child shouldn't have to worry about details like getting to the exam in time or how to get home from an exam.

If you can, take some time off work for at least the first few days of the exams. Your child will appreciate having you to come home to. You can have a good meal ready and an ear for listening.

Keep up the usual study routine this week and continue to urge your child to eat well and get lots of sleep. Discourage over-study at this stage: 'all-nighter' study sessions are never a good idea.

Ask your child if they have all the supplies they will need for the exams like calculator, set squares etc. Consult the Exam Equipment guide in Chapter 17, 'Before, during and after exams' and make sure your child has all these supplies. If not, get them! Your child must not turn up without these items. Doing so will add to their stress levels and will be very distracting. They may even be unable to do a particular question properly without the right equipment.

The day of the exam

Before the exam

- Get your child up nice and early on the morning of the exam and cook them a healthy, energy-friendly breakfast, preferably eggs (see Chapter 1, 'Keeping well' for ideas on breakfast).
- Make your child a healthy packed lunch or make sure they have enough money to buy lunch later. Give them lots of water for the exam and any chewy sweets he or she may like. Chewing a sweet in the exam can be good for concentration.
- Your child may not want to talk much this morning. That is perfectly understandable. Just keep up some mundane commentary about the weather, food etc. to fill in those awkward silences but don't hound your child to talk about the exam.
- However, you can remind them briefly of all the hard work they have done and that you expect only that they now do their best. Don't forget to tell them how proud you are of them already.
- Make sure your child leaves the house in plenty of time. They need to get to the exam centre early, at least 15 minutes before each exam. Rushing at this stage can be very stressful, so leave lots of time for getting there if you are driving. Otherwise, make sure they are in plenty of time for the bus.

Wish them luck and remind them again that this exam is not going to determine their entire life.

After the exam

Speak to your child as soon after the exam as possible. If you can't be at home, call them on the phone. Even if you have a sullen teenager who would die rather than let you know they are glad you called, they will be secretly happy you are interested. Phoning immediately afterwards tells your child that you have been thinking about them and that you are aware of the time of the exams. This level of interest in your child's activities is always positive.

Rather than launching into a series of questions about the content of the exam, which might be quite disheartening for your child, you could begin with a more general question like 'How do you feel?' This let's your child know that you are more interested in how they are than on their performance in the exam.

Allow your child to talk as little or as much about the exam as they want. Some will talk lots while others might only give you a 'Fine'. Either way, don't push your daughter or son into talking about it and never, never let yourself get engaged in a post-mortem of the exam. Don't pick the paper apart and certainly don't criticise what your son or daughter have written, if they tell you some things they wrote down that you don't think were correct. You or your child can't change anything now and pointing out negative things will serve no other purpose than to dent your child's confidence. Find only the positives and emphasise these.

If your child happens to be upset after the exam, reassure them that they did their best and encourage them now to put that exam behind them and move on. Urge them to take a couple of hours off, if they are tempted to launch straight back into study for the next exam. If they continue to be upset, put them in contact with their teacher or principal, who can often point out the positives on the paper.

Make sure that they eat well after the exam and once again get organised for the next one. Allow them time alone and encourage them to do something relaxing to wind down like watch some TV or take a walk.

Whatever you do, be there for your child in whatever capacity he or she wants and stay positive. You know your child best of all and you'll know what he or she needs.

Dos and don'ts for parents

Do	Don't
Create a study-friendly environment.	Nag.
Offer encouragement and support.	Impose your own ambitions on your child.
Facilitate routine.	Crowd your child.
Give rewards.	Allow all-night study sessions.
Keep your child healthy.	Think reading magazines is negative.
Stay informed.	Be negative.
Be positive.	

Section 2

Getting Organised to Study: Guide for Students

Getting organised to study means creating the best circumstances and the best frame of mind in which to learn. This involves keeping your body and mind healthy, getting a study space ready, motivating yourself to learn and arranging your time.

What you will learn in Section 2

This section shows you how to:
- keep well while you are studying
- create a study-friendly environment
- set up good study and practice habits
- motivate yourself to work hard
- manage your time.

1 Keeping well

It's important that you keep well in order to be able to study properly. This means staying healthy and fit while you go through the school year. Balancing study and leisure, staying fit, eating well and getting enough rest will all help maintain a healthy body and mind.

Eating well

The importance of eating healthy foods cannot be overemphasised. While the advantages to your general health are obvious, eating the right foods can be of huge benefit to your brain. Eating well can help prevent dehydration, help maintain concentration and provide positive energy for study and exams. Your mood, motivation and mental performance are all influenced by what you eat so it's essential to watch your diet while you study.

Cut out the junk

The most important change to make to your diet it to cut out junk food and drinks that provide what is called 'false energy'. This means that they may give you a sugar boost for a short time but, in fact, this is short lived and has no real positive benefit to your energy levels or concentration.

So, for the most part, try to avoid crisps, bars, biscuits, sweets and fizzy drinks. Replace them instead with nuts, fruit, some of the healthier breakfast bars and fruit juices or smoothies. These can be good options for snacks in your study or school breaks and you will begin to see a lot more long-term benefits than with the junk food. You will find that you won't get tired as quickly and you will have more energy overall. And your brain will thank you with more concentration capacity and energy.

You might be tempted to have meals that don't provide much nutritional value either. So you're better off without things like pizzas, chips and burgers and breakfast rolls. Instead, try to have healthier meals that will keep the body fit and the mind active.

Fruit and vegetables are hugely important in your diet, so try to eat as much as you can – aim for at least five servings per day – and mix and match a good variety of different types.

What to drink

If you're thirsty, drink water – it's better for your skin and your teeth and it won't give you the false energy you might get from sugary drinks.

Water also allows you to stay 'hydrated'. You need to stay hydrated in order to keep the brain functioning at its best. As soon as you begin to get dehydrated, the brain begins to lose concentration capacity. So, always carry a bottle of water with you to school and drink regularly throughout the day. While you study at home, keep the water beside you too. It is recommended that about 84 ounces of water a day is a good guide but the secret is really just to keep drinking at regular intervals.

If you can, avoid fizzy drinks, coffee and conventional tea, which all contain caffeine. While caffeine may give you a quick buzz when you first drink it, when you start to take in too much caffeine, you can become dehydrated and this is very bad for the brain capacity. Caffeine also dehydrates the body so try to limit your intake of this to small amounts per day.

Avoid conventional tea or coffee as much as you can, especially late in the evening and go for fruit juices or herbal teas instead; green tea is a good option for mental relaxation.

Eat regularly

It's vital to get into the habit of eating regularly – no skipping meals. Hunger is the enemy of study because when you're hungry concentration levels drop and you simply can't concentrate on learning – you'll be too busy thinking about how hungry you are!

Eat breakfast if you can

Breakfast is particularly important and it's a good idea to get into the habit of never skipping it. You need to start your day off well with good brain food, which doesn't mean stopping off at the local petrol station for a breakfast roll. So, a couple of times a week, eat eggs for breakfast and they are especially good on the morning of exams. Eggs are renowned as great brain food, because they provide lots of energy and help maintain concentration. Alternative breakfasts, when you don't have eggs, can include toast and marmalade, healthy cereal (such as porridge), fruit and yoghurt and brown bread.

Dinner

For dinner, aim for a balance of protein, fibre and some carbohydrates and fats. Fish is the most important brain food you could eat. It has high energy levels and has been proven to contribute to concentration levels and brain capacity. Salmon, sardines, trout, tuna, herring and mackerel all are excellent but avoid breaded fish and fish fingers. Go for fresh fish as often as possible. Other good options are beef, chicken, turkey and pork. If you are vegetarian, make sure you get enough protein by eating lentils, pulses and other beans. Eggs are also good at this time of the day, if you haven't already had them for breakfast.

Always try to include fresh vegetables in your dinner, especially the green ones like spinach, cabbage and broccoli. Find out what vegetables you like – there are loads to choose from – sweetcorn, frozen beans, carrots, cauliflower – and try to vary them every day.

Lunch

For lunch, you could try to get into the habit of eating a salad with some dairy produce - low fat cheeses, cottage cheese, yoghurt – wholemeal bread, pitta bread, omelette, and lots and lots of fruit.

If you have any doubt about what you should or shouldn't be eating, check with someone who knows well, like your Home Economics teacher, your doctor or a nutritionist.

Combating the common enemy

The common enemy of the student is the cold or flu. Not only will it mean missing time at school but your whole ability to work will have to be put on hold for maybe up to two weeks while you battle the cold or flu.

Vitamin C is the best preventative weapon you can use against this enemy, so aim to get lots of this vitamin into your diet. You'll find Vitamin C in foods like fresh fruits (especially blackcurrants and citrus fruits), peppers, green vegetables and freshly squeezed orange juice.

If you feel you are still not getting enough Vitamin C, check with your doctor – you may need to take Vitamin C supplements in the form of tablets or a tonic.

Balanced eating at a glance

Your aim at meal times should be to have a well-balanced meal, which means including foods that contain all the different nutrients in the right proportions. This simplified table of four different food groups should help you out. Aim to have at least one food from each group in each meal.

Table 1.1: Four food groups

Protein Group	Carbohydrate Group
Meat	Bread
Fish	Cereal
Eggs	Rice
Cheese	Pasta
Nuts	Potato
Vegetables	
Dairy Group	**Protective Group**
Milk	Fruit
Cheese	Vegetables
Yoghurt	

A note for the girls

Iron is a very important mineral in the body. If you don't get enough iron, you may suffer anaemia, which is often referred to as feeling 'run-down'. We lose iron when we bleed, so girls lose a lot of iron each month during their periods. This can lead to feelings of tiredness and dizziness, which will not be good for overall health and will be especially bad for brain capacity and concentration.

So you need to be aware of this and take in lots of iron. The best foods for iron are meat (especially liver) and green vegetables. If you feel you are still not getting enough iron, check with your doctor as you might need to take iron supplements in the form of tablets or a tonic.

Exercise regularly

Aim for at least 30 minutes of exercise time each day. This will help keep not just your body in good shape but will keep the mind healthy as well. Staying physically active eases tension, aids concentration and gives you more energy and stamina.

Walking is excellent for exercise, but you can also try cycling, football, hockey, tennis, badminton – in fact, anything that gets you away from the desk and physically active.

Yoga is also a great option if you feel particularly stressed. It will keep you fit and relieve the stress. Join a local class or buy a yoga DVD to exercise along with.

How to relieve stress and tension

Often when you sit at a desk for too long (and especially if you slouch over the desk) you'll notice that your neck and back become tight and tense. Or if you're writing a lot, your fingers and wrists may get cramped. So, it's a good idea to take a few moments to do some gentle and simple exercises to relieve this tension. Not only does this help ease tension in the short run but you'll save yourself some serious back problems in later life.

You may sometimes feel overwhelmed with work and begin to get stressed and find it difficult to concentrate. Taking a break at this stage and doing some gentle and slow exercises will help clear your mind and refocus.

Here are some exercises you can try when you're on your study breaks (or need a break). You don't need to aim to do them all together – do as many or as few as you think necessary – perhaps do the neck ones on one break and the wrist ones on another and so on.

For your neck
1   Sit up straight in your chair, staring directly ahead.
2   Move your head slowly as far around to the right as you can, hold for five seconds and move back slowly to the centre.
3   Now move your head to the left as far as you can, hold for five seconds and move back to the centre.
4   Repeat up to ten times on each side.
5   Begin again at the staring ahead position.
6   Tip your head down towards your left shoulder, hold for five seconds and come back up to the centre. Do the same towards the right shoulder.
7   Repeat up to ten times on each side.
8   Back to the starting position, move your head around and look over your right shoulder as far as you can.
9   Hold for five seconds and move back to the centre.

10 Do the same over the left shoulder and repeat up to ten times on each side.
11 Finally, roll your head clockwise and anti-clockwise three times in each direction.

For your back and shoulders

1 Begin by sitting straight on the chair again, feet planted on the floor.
2 Place your right arm down by your side and grip under the chair with your right hand.
3 Hold onto the chair with your right hand and lean over to your left side as far as you can, and hold for five seconds.
4 Move back up to the original position.
5 Repeat this five times.
6 Now change to the other side, gripping the chair this time with your left hand. Lean to the right and hold for five seconds and then move back to the centre.
7 Repeat five times.
8 Stand up now, feet planted about shoulder-width apart, arms hanging loosely by your sides.
9 Now raise both arms up slowly over your head and reach up as far as you can (keep your eyes staring directly ahead), and hold for five seconds.
10 Lower your arms slowly back down to your sides.
11 Repeat up to ten times.
12 Begin again standing straight and with arms to the side.
13 Bend your arms at the elbow and hold them loosely.
14 Twist your body, from the waist around to the left side, move slowly back to the centre and then twist around to the right.
15 Repeat this process up to ten times.
16 Standing straight and staring ahead again with arms hanging loosely by your side, scrunch up your shoulders to your neck as tight as you can. Hold for five seconds and then let them relax fully.
17 Repeat up to ten times.
18 Loosen out your shoulders and arms by shaking them around for a few seconds.

For your fingers and wrists

1 Hold your arms out loosely in front of you.
2 Stretch out all your fingers on both hands as much as you can and then scrunch them into a tight fist.
3 Repeat this up to ten times.
4 With the palms facing you, put all the fingers together in each hand.

5   Now take the right thumb and place it against the bottom part of the right little finger; the left thumb at the left little finger. Hold for five seconds.

6   Repeat this up to ten times.

7   Again with the palms facing you, press each of the tips of every finger against the thumb on that hand. Make sure you keep the fingers straight while you're doing this.

8   Holding your hands in loose fists with the thumbs facing you, slowly tilt your hands to the right as far as you can, hold for five seconds and shift back to the centre.

9   Tilt now to the left as far as you can, hold for five seconds and back to the centre. Repeat this up to ten times.

10 Keeping your hands in loose fists and with thumbs facing you, twist your hands around in each direction as far as you can. Repeat up to ten times.

11 To loosen out your fingers and wrists, relax your fingers and shake your hands vigorously from the wrist for a few seconds.

Maintaining a healthy balance

It might seem like strange advice to tell you that the best way to stay focused on study is to get away from it, but it's true. You need to keep a healthy balance of study and leisure. When you get away from learning for a while and do something fun, you'll find yourself refreshed and ready to work hard when you get back. So build leisure time into your schedule and you won't regret it.

Sleeping well

Sleep is of the most crucial importance at any time in your life, but particularly when you need to be at your best mentally. If you let yourself get too tired, your brain will slow down, your concentration will not be good and even your whole mood and outlook will suffer.

How much sleep is enough?

Aim to get eight hours of sleep every night. This should include a few hours of a 'good night's sleep', which is time in bed before midnight. The sleep you get before midnight is particularly beneficial, so going to bed at 3 a.m. and sleeping until 11 a.m. is not a good sleep – you need to get at least a couple of hours before midnight for the best sleep value.

What if you're having trouble sleeping?

Have you ever gone to bed, looking forward to a good night's sleep, but your mind has kept racing – perhaps with all the information you've acquired that day, or with worries about how much more work you need to do? Here I explain ways you can clear your mind and relax so that your body will wind down and you can sleep.

One good way to clear your mind and relax is to take some gentle exercise after you study, like a short walk. If you have an MP3 player, bring it with you and listen to some music as you walk and you should feel yourself relaxing. This will also help make you physically tired as well as being mentally tired from study.

You can then top off the relaxation with some TV and a hot bath before bed and you should be well on your way to dream world.

However, if you still find your mind racing in bed, keep a pad of paper and a pen beside your bed. This way you can jot down anything you want to remember the next day and you won't be kept awake worrying that you'll forget it in the morning.

In order to relax the mind and body, you can also do a relaxation exercise to clear your brain and relax your muscles. Try this one:

1   Lie flat on your back.
2   Place all your concentration and focus to your toes.
3   Now imagine there are weights hanging from each toe pulling them down into the bed.
4   When you feel your toes relaxing, concentrate on your ankles.
5   Imagine weights hanging from these pulling them down into the mattress.
6   When you feel the muscles relax move up to your calves.
7   Continue to repeat this process all the way up your body – although it's highly unlikely you'll get to your head, as you'll be asleep by then.

If you're still experiencing problems sleeping, you might want to try some meditation, which can clear the mind, relax the body and help ease stress and tension, as well as putting you into a more positive frame of mind. Do a search on the internet for beginner's meditation techniques or buy a CD or DVD as a guide.

Some quick dos and don't for keeping well

Do	Don't
Eat healthy food.	Skip meals.
Drink lots of water.	Live on junk food.
Exercise regularly.	Drink lots of caffeine.
Sleep well.	Forget the leisure side of life.
Relieve tension with exercise.	

2 Setting the scene: creating a study-friendly environment

It's vital that you create a study-friendly atmosphere. Sometimes it's very difficult to concentrate on learning, so it will help if you set a scene for yourself that is free from distractions and has all you need around you. I outline how you can do this below.

Study in the same place and at the same time every day

If you study in the same place every day, this helps create the habit of study and has the added advantage of being less distracting. It also means that you can have all your materials in one place and not have to haul them back and forth between different places.

You should also study at about the same time each day – again to get into the habit of doing so. This will also become a time when your family know you study and they'll know to leave you alone!

Set up a desk

It is always best to have a desk (or at least a table) and comfortable chair for study. Make sure you set them up in a quiet, well-lit, well-ventilated place. Many students try to study at the kitchen or dining-room table but this is generally not a good idea. These are often busy rooms and are therefore too distracting. Your bedroom, a study room or spare room is probably best.

Make sure you have good lighting, preferably a reading lamp, on your desk. Be aware of room temperature as well: too hot and you'll want to sleep; too cold and it will be tough to concentrate.

Of course, you may not have access to a quiet room at home. If this is a problem, then try the supervised study option in your school. This can be a very good way to make yourself study. This time is supervised, so there will be no talking allowed and basically you will have no choice but to work.

Get rid of all distractions

TV, radio, MP3 players and mobile phones will distract you. Make sure you turn them all off and lay them aside for your study time.

You may have heard of research that suggests listening to music can aid learning. I disagree. Think about this: if you are humming the song you are listening to then you cannot be concentrating fully on study.

Have on hand all necessary supplies

Have everything you need for your study with you when you sit down. Bring the appropriate books from school and always have a supply of paper, folders, pens, pencils, calculator, highlighters etc. on your desk.

Your study area might look something like this:

2.1 Typical study desk

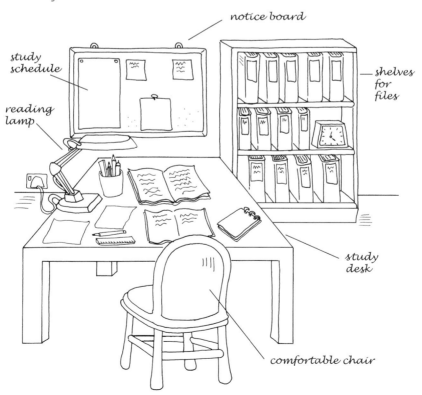

Keep this list of supplies you'll need for your study tasks in mind:

- Pens and pencils
- Ruler
- Maths equipment like calculator, protractor, compass, etc.
- Highlighters
- Paper clips and stapler with staples
- Ring binders
- A4 dividers
- A4 hole-punched refill pad
- Hole puncher
- Cue cards and filing box with dividers
- Eraser
- Pencil sharpener
- Dictionaries
- Thesaurus.

3 Forming good study habits

Studying is all about developing good habits and, most importantly, those good habits should include planning and practice.

Start early

Start your learning and study as early as you can. The more time you have, the less stress you'll be under. However, don't think that it's now too late. Just figure out how many months/weeks you have left, make out a list of high-priority tasks you need to get done in that time and take it from there.

Don't count on June

Don't think that you'll get lots of study done at the end of May/beginning of June. Don't take one look at your exam timetable, see that something like Chemistry is not until the end with lots of free days in between and think you'll learn it then. Remember, sitting exams will be an exhausting experience and you'll be way too tired to learn a pile of new work at this stage. Leave the days in between exams for recaps only of material you already know.

Keep in mind too that usually the weather in those first two weeks in June is the best of the year. With the sun shining outside, you'll find concentration very difficult, so begin your learning early in the year and aim to be finished all new material by the end of April.

Take responsibility

You must take responsibility for your own study. No one can do the work for you. You might be tempted to blame a 'bad' teacher – don't fall into this trap. Just accept whatever situation you find yourself in and decide that you're the one who has to do the work.

So use this guide to sit down and figure out what you need to do to plan your approach to study, what your aims are, and how you are going to achieve them.

Plan your study

Always plan your study well. Decide what you want to do, estimate the time it will take you to do it and then assign a time for doing it. (You will can find out about the best way to timetable in Chapter 5 below.) Keep a list of your homework and a weekly list of other revision tasks you would like to complete that week. Keep it realistic and stick to it.

However, don't worry too much if you don't stick perfectly to your plan every week. Life happens and sometimes things will occur during the week to disrupt your plans. Just readjust your schedule and continue on. Scheduling is always important but doesn't have to be carved in stone.

Reward yourself

Give yourself rewards as you go along. Take regular breaks and at the end of study sessions treat yourself to something nice for work well done. Promise yourself that if you complete a certain amount of work, you will then go out with your friends or watch a movie.

Use memory tricks

Make use of memory tricks like flash cards, pictures and acronyms in your learning. Mix and match them into your notes and use them for material you are finding it difficult to retain. You will learn more about memory tricks in Chapter 9 below.

Review your work regularly

It's no good just learning something once. You'll forget it (we all will!). But you will increase your chances of remembering something every time you review it, or go back over it, so review things you learn frequently. Review what you've learned at different stages:

- 10 minutes after learning
- 1 day after learning
- 1 week after learning
- 1 month after learning
- 6 months after learning.

Stick to this as much as you can, but the main message is to continue to review work throughout the year.

Mix tasks

Switch subjects after breaks. This is important because it stops you from doing too much on your favourite subjects and less on your least favourite ones. You need to give all subjects fairly equal attention. Also, it's a good idea to switch tasks regularly from some writing to some reading, some committing to memory to some note taking.

Note also that it's a good idea to leave aside for a while a task that isn't going well. If you feel yourself getting bogged down in a task that you just can't handle and you're getting frustrated, put it aside for a while. Complete another simpler task off your list and then come back to the difficult one. Quite often when we come back refreshed to it we can see where we were going wrong. If you're still struggling, don't be afraid to admit it and ask for help from your teacher.

Listen to teachers

Always read back over your teacher's comments on your homework and try to incorporate any advice he or she might have given you into the next answer. Never dismiss your teacher's comments as anti-student or something like that; you could miss out on some good advice.

Leave the best for last

Try to leave your favourite subject to the end of your study session. At this time you will probably be getting a little tired and fed up, so if you've left your least favourite subject until now, it will be tempting to not bother. However, if you're facing your favourite subject, it will be easier to keep going.

Recognise your strengths and weaknesses

Learn to recognise where your strengths and weaknesses are in study time. Enhance your strengths and aim to fix the weaknesses. Do you have a particularly difficult subject that you're struggling with? Then get help. Do you find that the same thing distracts you every day? Then work on doing something about it.

Avoid new material late in the game

When you get nearer the exams, make decisions on what sections you want to answer in certain subjects and concentrate on learning these well. Avoid new material at this stage and practise what you now know you will need.

4 Motivating yourself: strategies

If you were about to go out and play a football final, the team coach would give you what's called a 'pep talk'. He or she would remind you perhaps of how well you played in the semi-final, tell you how well you *can* play, remind you that the opposing team beat you last time, and so on. All this, the coach hopes, will 'psyche you up' to play your very best.

In a similar way, you must motivate yourself to study. You need to believe in yourself and have an aim in mind. This will help keep you at the study desk. Here are a few strategies to consider.

Same place, same time

Creating the habit of study in the same place and at the same time each evening is good for motivation. You know that when you sit at that desk at that time, you always study.

Keep your work area tidy

Always keep your work area tidy and organised. Take a few moments at the end of every study session to file away sheets of paper and tidy your desk. It'll be a lot easier coming back to it if you don't have to tidy first.

This will also make it a lot easier to find what you're looking for – it can be frustrating to have to search through mounds of paper for a list you know you had a few days ago but is buried somewhere mysterious now. You'll probably be tempted to give up if you can't lay your hands on it immediately, so don't allow this to happen.

Begin positively

Begin each learning session by reciting something you have already learned. This positive experience makes you feel good and spurs you onto further learning.

Alternatively, pin up over your desk a recent test in which you did really well – the reminder of this high mark can help you achieve more success.

Complete a task

Have a 'to-do list' of tasks on hand and complete one of the tasks. Tick it off your to-do list and you'll feel a great sense of achievement.This will spur you on to more achievements.

Keep planning

Keep planning ahead. When you have one list completed, work out your tasks for the next week. This will help you to feel organised and on top of things. You'll also see that you're progressing and that's great for morale.

Use motivation signs

Make out a motivation sign to put over your desk. This inspires you and sets a goal. These goals could be short term, like 'Finish three chapters of geography this week', or long term, like 'I want to go to college'. What you think will be a goal for you is, of course, up to you and depends on your own ambitions. But do set goals – aiming to achieve targets will keep you trying.

Figure 4.1: Sample motivation signs

Share problems

Feeling alone and isolated can be very bad for your motivation, so make sure you share frustrations and worries with people who'll understand like your friends, parents, teachers or school counsellor. Finding out that others are feeling just as stressed can be reassuring and set you on the path to study again.

Study in a group

It can be very beneficial to study as part of a group:

■ It can help you set tasks and share frustrations.
■ Access to others people's ideas can be invaluable.
■ It can motivate you to finish tasks for the next meeting of the group.

However, groups can also be dangerous, as they can be very distracting and can turn into a chatting session rather than a study group. If you're going to be part of a study group it needs to be just that. Follow these simple rules to keep the group on track:

1   Be determined that the group is there for study and not chat.
2   Meet only with people you can trust to stick to Rule 1.
3   Set a time and place to meet on regular occasions, like maybe every Saturday afternoon from 2:00 to 3:15.
4   Arrive on time; if you arrive late it can be very distracting for others and they'll have to stop to update you or if they don't you'll feel lost.
5   Use your first meeting to decide what subjects/topics the group will concentrate on for the next few weeks.
6   Assign a set task to each person whose job it'll be to do the task and report back to the group the next week. End every other meeting this way also. Each person there should go away with a set task to complete.
7   Allow 5 minutes at the beginning of the meeting for general chat. After the 5 minutes, get down to work. Have each person 'teach' the others what they learned from their task or show the group how to answer a question etc.
8   Make sure everyone takes a turn.
9   Everyone should feel free to ask questions, even if they seem to be stupid ones. You shouldn't laugh at anyone else's stupid question; your question next week could be even more stupid!
10 End the meeting with assigning the new tasks.

5 Time to study: organising your study schedule

The importance of organising your time cannot be overemphasised. Nobody wants to spend all their time studying, so it's best to make the most of the time you do lay aside for that purpose. It's also vital that you allow yourself time to do other things that you like doing – sport, reading, music, or just relaxing.

Of course, organising your time will take practice but if you stick with it, it becomes easier. You need to sort out when you will study each day, what you will study, allow time for recreation and fit in all your homework too.

Daily timetable

First, let's look at fitting in your study around the rest of your life. When I talk about study time here, this includes homework and learning time.

Make out a timetable of everything you do all day and put in the times when you would like to do your study and homework. This gives you an idea of how much time you can allot to your work and when you have the time to do so.

Your timetable might look something like this:

Table 5.1: Daily timetable

Time	Activity
8:00–9:00	Get up and get ready for school.
9:00–15:30	School.
15:30–16:30	Journey home and dinner.
16:30–17:00	Relax, watch TV.
17:00–20:00	Homework and study.
20:20–21:20	Football practice.
21:30–10:30	TV.
10:30	Bed.

Of course, on Saturday and Sunday, you can decide for yourself how much time you want to assign to study.

Homework schedule

One of the major issues for anyone working towards an exam in school is the problem of completing assigned homework and fitting in learning and revision time too. You can do this though by dividing up your homework into more manageable smaller tasks that won't take as much time.

Let's face it, if on Tuesday you get ten questions in Physics to complete for Friday, some of you would be tempted to leave them until Thursday. But by Thursday, ten questions will take up a lot of your time and where will you find the time to do all the other homework for Thursday night? The best way to avoid this is to do a little of this homework on Tuesday night, a little on Wednesday and the rest on Thursday.

Estimating your time is important for planning and for giving yourself an idea of when you might be finished your work. Take a look at this sample homework schedule for a Monday night showing how you can break your homework down over different nights:

Do each question as if you were doing it in an exam

Table 5.2: Sample homework schedule

Subject	Homework	Due	Time Needed	Schedule
Maths	Learn theorem, p.5	2moro	20 mins	Tonight.
Geography	6 2s on erosion	Wed	40 mins	Tonight: 2s 1-3 (20 mins). Tues: 2s 3-6 (20 mins).
Home Economics	12 2s on home finance	Fri	$1^1/_2$ hrs	Tonight: 2s 1-4 (20 mins). Tues: 2s 5-8 (20 mins). Wed: 2s 9-12 (20 mins). Thurs: Revise & learn (30 mins).
French	Letter, p.52	2moro	40 mins	Tonight

Keep all homework in a pile
If not up to standard go back to teach

You can complete this type of schedule in your homework journal. If you don't have a journal, then make sure you get a notebook to keep track of homework assigned and keep track of what you have and have not completed.

The **first column** gives the subject and the **second column** the homework assigned for that night. The **due column** shows you when you need to submit that homework. Into the **time needed** column you will estimate how long it will take you to complete that homework. You may find this tough at first, but once you get used to estimating, it will become more accurate. If you practise this for a few weeks, you will probably notice that it takes you about the same time each night to do a certain subject.

When you have a subject that is not due for a few days and will take you quite a lot of time, it is a good idea to divide that homework over two or three nights. You will see on the sample schedule that this has been done in the case of Home Economics and Geography and the information has been filled in the **schedule** column. You'll also notice that if you do a few questions per night in Home Economics, there is time left on Thursday night to revise and learn those answers to the questions given. This is a way in which you can incorporate some extra study time into your homework schedule.

So, when you go home and sit down to do your homework, take your highlighter and highlight all the homework that you have scheduled for tonight. (Don't forget to check back on previous days to see if you had anything scheduled from another day to complete tonight.) In my example, it is estimated that about 1 hour and 40 minutes will be spent on these tasks. Now, depending on how long you like to spend on your study, you will have time to do other learning or revision tasks.

Study 'to-do' list

Now that you have managed to allow time for other study and learning tasks, you should always have a 'to-do' list. This is a list of those tasks you would like to complete in any given week. For this purpose, it's always a good idea to have a weekly list of things you would like to get achieved, over and above your usual homework.

This means that when you are finished your homework and feel you would like to do some extra study, you check your prepared list to see what you will do. You don't want to be wasting your precious time deciding what to do – a to-do list saves this dilemma.

The most important thing to keep in mind is to keep your to-do list very specific. Lay out exact tasks. Don't be vague about what you want to achieve. For example, you might want to 'get some Geography done this week.' That's not specific enough. It's better to aim for something like: 'learn the five types of Mechanical Weathering.'

A to-do list of tasks might look something like this:

Table 5.3: Weekly list of tasks		
Subject	**Topics**	**Estimated time**
Business Studies	Communications:	
	– Introduction	20 mins
	– Barriers to Communication	15 mins
	– Internal v External Comm.	20 mins
Geog.	Patterns and Processes in Physical Environment:	
	– Tectonic Cycle	45 mins
	– Rock Cycle	50 mins
	– Landform Development	30 mins

For this type of list, you will also need to look at revision tasks you need to go back over and learn. The most important thing to remember is to keep your weekly list *realistic*. This is essential for your own self-esteem. It can be very satisfying to finish a list of tasks you've assigned yourself but quite soul destroying to not get even half of it completed. So be sensible about how much you think you can achieve in one week. You can always add to your list if you get everything done before the end of the week.

It's a good idea to break large topics into smaller sections, mainly because you don't want tasks that will take up too much time at one sitting and also, it will be a lot easier to remember less notes. Again you need to estimate how long it will take you to do each learning task.

So when you are finished your homework and feel you would like to do some extra study, you only have to check your prepared list to see what you will do.

The most important thing about scheduling your study time is to stay organised and keep track of tasks you complete and those you still need to do. Be aware that you need to make the most of your time. Don't let 'free classes' slip by without doing some study and if you have a free 20 minutes before your favourite TV programme, don't waste it – go back over your Chemistry notes. Use time efficiently.

Study in 45-minute blocks

Generally, the average concentration time on one task is 45 minutes. It can be difficult to continue to study after this, so study in 45-minute blocks.

Take 5-10 minute breaks

Once your 45 minutes are up, take a 5- or 10-minute break. This allows your mind time to rest and recharge and allows you to get up and have a walk around, a snack or drink. Be careful though and only take the allotted minutes (don't get distracted by TV and let your 5-minute break turn into a 30-minute one).

Review work completed

Before beginning your next task after your break take a quick review back over what you did in the previous 45 minutes. Ask yourself, 'what did I learn before the break?' and try and recite the main points of what you learned.

Switch subjects

After your review, it is a good idea to switch subjects, if you can. This can help stem off boredom and it prevents you from concentrating only on your favourite subjects. It's a good idea to start with your least favourite or most difficult subject first. That way you get it out of the way and you are not leaving it to the end, when you might be tired and tempted to not do it at all.

Some quick dos and don'ts of getting organised to study

Do	Don't
Mind yourself physically and mentally.	Waste time.
Create a study-friendly environment.	Give up.
Stay motivated.	Dismiss planning and scheduling as a waste of time.
Schedule your study.	Wait until June!
Keep a list of tasks to do.	

Section 3

'Taking It All In'

You spend a lot of your time at school, plenty of time doing homework and more time studying for exams. How can you make sure you take it all in?

This section will show you how to absorb information effectively so that you can use it later – for schoolwork and exams.

What you will learn in Section 3

In this section, you will learn about:
- reading skills
- listening skills
- note-taking skills
- memory tricks.

6 The root of all learning: reading skills

Almost all learning begins with reading. You read something, you learn it, and you give it back in exams.

'Well, that's easy,' you might say, 'I already know how to read.'

But while we may think we can read well, reading to study and learn is very different from reading a favourite magazine for entertainment. In order to learn, you need to develop reading skills that will help you achieve that end.

Specifically, you need to **read to learn** and **read to answer questions**.

Reading to learn strategies

It would be impossible to learn every word you read, so when you read to learn, your aim is to find the most important information and convey that to memory.

Do a quick survey of the chapter

Prepare yourself for learning by surveying what you need to read. A quick survey can give you an overall idea of what you will be learning and what the important areas are. Skim through the introduction, the headings and sub-headings and the conclusion/summary of the text.

Ask yourself questions

The best way to learn is to answer questions you have set yourself. When you have to find answers to questions, learning becomes more focused on what's important.

Asking questions will also help you keep your concentration on what you are reading and engage you with the text. This will make you more interested in what you're reading and go a long way to combating the dreaded distractions.

To come up with the right questions, turn the section headings into questions. For example, imagine a heading for a section in your Business Studies book is 'The Functions of a Bank', then your question could be 'What are the functions of a bank?'

If there are questions at the end of a chapter or section, you can use these to focus your study.

Find the answers: scanning

Often you will not have to read everything to find your answer. You can simply **scan** for the answer. This will help you focus on certain information, rather than trying to take everything in.

You scan by deciding what information you are looking for and then quickly looking for the answer. For instance, you can spot some answers by looking for capital letters to locate names and places or by looking for dates. For example, if one of your questions is 'When did Christopher Columbus discover America?' then all you have to do is scan for a date. If you're looking for the names of his ships, they will most likely be printed in bold or italic in the book. This will allow you to spot important information and you won't have to read all the text around it.

Highlight important information

Based on the questions you are using, you might want to highlight or underline the answers. However, a word of warning: it is easy to go a bit crazy with the highlighter and have entire sections highlighted. It's usually better to read through the entire section first (often points are stated more than once), and then highlight only the key words and phrases that will help jog your memory.

Write your questions and answers

Write out your questions and answers. Try to state the answers in your own words, rather than in the exact words of the author and keep answers as brief and to the point as possible.

Recite information

Once you have finished reading and answered all your questions, go back and ask yourself the questions again. Try to give the answers without looking at what you have written. If you can't, read the answer again. Repeat this process until you can answer all the questions without your written notes.

Review learning

Always review what you've learned regularly. Never presume that because you've learned it once, you will always remember what you've read. Go back over the questions and try to fill in the answers on regular occasions. Begin by reviewing the next day, then the next week, then the next month, then two months later and so on, until you have to review all your work before the exam.

> ## Reading to answer questions: strategies

Reading a passage and answering questions on a passage is a task you meet frequently in homework, tests and exams. This involves reading, understanding, finding information and forming opinions on a piece of writing. Developing the skill to deal well with this task involves simple strategies that you can perfect with practice.

Skim

Skimming means having a quick read through the passage once. This will give you a general idea of what the passage is about.

Read closely

To read closely, go back and read the passage again, carefully and slowly this time. A writer will usually make one main point or present one idea per paragraph. This is called the **subject line** or **topic sentence**.

So, if you want to make sure that you understand all the main points being made, you need to identify the topic sentence or subject line of each paragraph.

Have a look at this paragraph:

> **Though racing is traditionally regarded as a male domain, the school has been getting more female applicants than it can cope with.** 'Out of our possible maximum of 30 students, we only have living arrangements for six girls every year. And these beds have been constantly filled since we introduced them,' reports Paddy Duffy, the instructing supervisor. 'There are certainly more girls in the business than ever before and that's the direction it's headed.' There may be few enough currently battling with Charlie Swan, but there is a discernible levelling out of gender scales and it can only be a matter of time.

You will have worked out that in the paragraph above the topic sentence is in bold. This is the main point of the paragraph: that there are more female applicants to the racing school than they can currently cope with. The rest of the paragraph just backs up this point and explains it further.

Usually the topic sentence is the first sentence of the paragraph, but not always:

> It's a bit like being an aspiring footballer. If you're one of the lucky ones, you get taken on in your mid-teens by a northern or British club, swapping the familiar safety of your family for the alien hardship of training camp. Only your dreams are there to carry you through the daily slog. **And, as in racing, many are called but few are chosen for the Premier League.**

In this paragraph the topic sentence comes at the end because the main point is that many go through the training but few are chosen for the famous life.

So, when you want to find the most important information in the passage, look for the topic sentence(s).

Read the questions accurately

Your next step is to read carefully through all the questions you are asked to answer. Then take each question in turn and follow the procedure below for answering it.

Read the question again carefully and be very clear about what it is asking you to do. If the question just asks you to **list** items, then all you need to do is list them, not explain, or give your opinion or summarise the whole passage; just list.

Scan

Once you've decided that you know what the question is looking for, you need to scan the passage for the answer. As you know, this involves having a quick glance across the passage to find the paragraph(s) that contains the information you are looking for.

You can then have another read through this paragraph(s) to find your answer, which you might want to highlight. If it's going to be a long answer, you might find it useful to jot down some rough notes of what information you are finding.

When you scan for information, you might have to look for direct information or implied information.

Direct information consists of facts that you have to find and write down. For example, in a passage, you read that:

... mobile phone use has seen remarkable growth since the nineties. In the five years between 1995 and 2000, the number of mobile users in Europe increased from less than 3 million to over 60 million. Mobile calls now account for over half of all telephone use.

The question here might be, *'How much did mobile phone use increase in the years between 1995 and 2000?'* To answer this question you simply have to find the statistic about increased mobile phone use, which involves taking direct information from the passage: *'It increased from less than 3 million to over 60 million users.'*

Looking for **implied information** can be a little more challenging. This is when the writer tells us certain things but is also suggesting other things that are not stated directly.

Consider this statement:

The story of the fatal ambush at Beal na mBlath, between Bandon and Macroom, on Tuesday evening, shows that the Commander-in-Chief fought heroically to the last, and then with his dying breath breathed into the ears of his comrades 'Forgive them'. These were the last words he uttered.

You are told very little in this short paragraph about the commander-in-chief, yet there is a lot of information *implied*. The fact that his final words are 'Forgive them' tells us a lot about him. It suggests he is brave, forgiving, heroic, religious, strong and selfless. The writer implies all these things when he just tells us about his last words. So, when you look for implied information, always ask yourself: what is the writer suggesting here?

You can also use implied information to form opinions. In this extract it is easy to form an opinion of the commander-in-chief by what is implied about him. You could say that you admire him because even at the moment of his death he was willing to forgive those who killed him. You could say you admire his bravery and willingness to stick to his religious beliefs about forgiving your enemy, even in such extreme circumstances.

Answer the questions

You are now ready to answer the questions. Use the sentences you have underlined and your rough notes to help. Make sure you answer the question fully (for example, if you are asked for reason**s**, always give more than one reason) and write in full sentences.

It is very important to keep your answers concise and to the point. Don't wander off into areas that are not questioned. **Stick to the question that's asked**. It is also important to develop your answer fully for maximum marks.

Consider this question, read the passage and then take a look at the answers that follow:

Question: How does the writer suggest that there is a lot of pent-up danger in the bull?

> Now, one year later, he was enormous. His neck, with it jutting humps of muscle, carried a head so huge that the eyes looked tiny. And there was nothing friendly in those eyes now; no expression at all, in fact, only a cold black glitter. Occasionally he snorted from deep in his chest but apart from that he remained frighteningly still. Monty wasn't just a bull – he was a giant.

Answer 1: *The writer suggests danger when he says the bull was 'frighteningly still'.*

Answer 2: *The writer suggests that there is a lot of pent-up danger in the bull when he tells us about his eyes. He says that they held no expression, just a cold black glitter, which implies, to me, danger. Again, the writer says that the bull was 'frighteningly still', suggesting tension and danger. The bull is unnaturally still and therefore expected to move dangerously at any moment. We also feel his power and strength when the writer mentions his 'jutting humps of muscle'.*

Both answers here are technically correct but the second answer would get the best marks. Why? Because it is a *fully developed* answer. Notice how the answer expands on all the points the student can find in the paragraph. The answer is clear, to the point and written in full sentences. Always make sure you do the same.

Some quick dos and don'ts of reading skills	
Do	**Don't**
Read with questions in mind.	Just read without thinking about what you're reading.
Take notes.	Answer in sentence fragments.
Stay engaged with your reading.	Wander off the point.
Answer questions fully.	Attempt questions without reading the passage fully first.
Answer the question that's asked.	

7 Learning to listen

Most of your learning begins in the classroom. Developing good listening skills in class, therefore, is an important first step down the road to study. If you can learn to listen in class, you can access important information quickly and be a step ahead when it comes to revising after class.

There is a big difference between *hearing* and *listening*. You hear things around you all the time: songs on the radio, conversations, gossip, instructions, but do you really listen? In order to listen to learn you need to firstly create the circumstances needed for effective listening and secondly to listen actively.

Creating the circumstances

Build a 'listening bubble'

There are many things that can distract us from listening. These are often referred to as 'barriers to listening'. In order to listen carefully you need to get rid of as many of these barriers as you can. This is known as building a **listening bubble**, in which you create the best possible opportunity for yourself to listen.

Be on time

You won't be in the right frame of mind to listen if you're late for class. Chances are you'll miss that first introduction by the teacher and you'll be lost from the outset, so aim to arrive in plenty of time.

Take up position

If you're able, position yourself in class with a clear view of the speaker – near the front of the room. It may be tempting to rush to the back row but here you will have too many distractions. If you have a clear view of the speaker, you will find it easier to stay focused on what he or she is saying.

Physical well-being

It's easy to be distracted by physical things like hunger or cold. So make sure you eat healthy food regularly. Have a good breakfast, a nourishing snack for morning break and a good lunch – no hunger pangs, no distraction. The same applies to body temperature. If you are regularly cold in class, wear some extra layers.

Take care also of any other physical discomforts you may encounter. Wear those glasses if you need them and tie back long hair that's hanging in your eyes. The simple rule is: if it's distracting and you can fix it, then fix it.

Mental well-being

Some distractions can be psychological. You've just had a row with your friend and now you can't stop thinking about it. This isn't going to help your listening skills. So sort out the row before class or make a conscious decision to deal with it later, and leave room in your head for lessons. Other problems may not be so easily resolved. So just tell yourself that you cannot do anything about them for this 35 minutes or 1 hour and push them to the back of your mind. Aim to stay focused on what is happening *now*.

Keep an open mind: give the speaker a chance

Keeping an open mind is vital. Often students are already turned off listening before they even come in the door. Prejudice against the speaker can be a huge barrier to listening. You've already decided that you don't like this teacher, or that teacher is useless, or the other teacher is boring. Listening is already doomed in this case.

Instead, go into each class with a fresh outlook. Presume that you will get something valuable out of each lesson and you usually will. Sometimes, it's a good idea to pretend you are reading a transcript of what is being said and you don't know who has written it. This will allow you to detach from the personality of the speaker and focus instead on what they are saying.

Be strong!

You may find that sometimes other students in class will distract you by talking or trying to catch your attention. Ignore them.

Don't sit beside them and soon they'll get the message and give up. Certainly, this kind of decision takes strength and bravery and you might get teased and called a 'swot', but who cares? It you don't react to this taunting, these other students will tire of it and realise you're serious about work. And you'll be proud of yourself for taking a stand. It is, after all, your exam and only you can determine to do well or not.

Active listening

If you want to listen effectively and learn in the process, it is not enough to just hear what's being said to you, you must engage in **active listening**. Active listening will help you adsorb information, categorise what's important and what's not and start the process of committing information to memory.

Prepare to listen

You are halfway to listening well if you know in advance what you are listening for. Review your class notes from the previous lesson and know where you left off. The teacher will usually be picking up at this point. You will therefore already know what to expect and you can listen out for it. Even better is to have a few questions prepared that you hope to hear the answers to. In this way you can listen carefully for the answers and jot them down.

Listen for 'buzz words'

It would be impossible to listen carefully to every single word the teacher says, so learn to spot the important information. Listen for the **buzz** words.

A teacher will usually preface important points with phrases like: 'To sum up', 'The three main reasons are…', 'In conclusion', 'To review', 'This is important', 'Remember that…', 'Keep in mind' and so on. Listen out for phrases like this and then focus carefully on what follows.

Take notes

If you jot down the important points a teacher makes, then you will listen carefully. Taking notes is essential to active listening. You don't need to write down every word. Again, listen out for the important phrases that will tell you an important point is to follow. Having to make these decisions about what is important and what's not keeps you focused on the class at hand.

Don't give up

Even when you are finding it toughgoing don't give up. Often you will find the information difficult to understand. But stick with it, continue to take notes and don't be afraid to ask the teacher for help at the end of class.

Some quick dos and don'ts of listening skills

Do	Don't
Decide to listen.	Let others distract you.
Actively listen by taking notes.	Go to class hungry or cold.
Review the previous lesson.	Allow outside distractions into your mind.
Give the teacher a chance.	Give up.

8 The art of note taking

You won't be able to get away from taking notes when you study. It would be impossible to learn entire textbooks and copies full of class work. As a result, your aim is to *reduce* the amount of material you need to learn. You do this by taking notes.

You use those notes to write down all the most important information you absolutely have to learn. The best notes will be organised, logical and concise.

Materials you need for note taking

A4 paper

Generally, it is advisable to take notes onto **A4, hole-punched** paper. Most students prefer A4 sheets because they can then organise them easily into A4 ring binders. It's a good idea to have one ring binder per subject, into which you put all your notes from that subject. This also makes it easy to slot in any handouts you may get and to add in more notes later, if necessary. Use dividers to break each subject folder into topics within that subject.

Cue cards

Alternatively, you may prefer to use small, lined cue cards (also called flash cards) for note taking. Many students find them easy to organise and handle. If you choose this option, again make sure you organise them into subjects and topics – you can get small boxes and dividers for this purpose.

Hard-back copy

However, many teachers will ask you to have a **hard-back copy** for note taking in class. If this is the case, you can keep all your notes here but make sure that *you leave some pages* after each note-taking session, to add in your own notes later.

Pens and highlighters

You will also need different coloured pens and highlighters when you take notes.

Organising the page for note taking

Figure 8.1: Page layout of the notes page

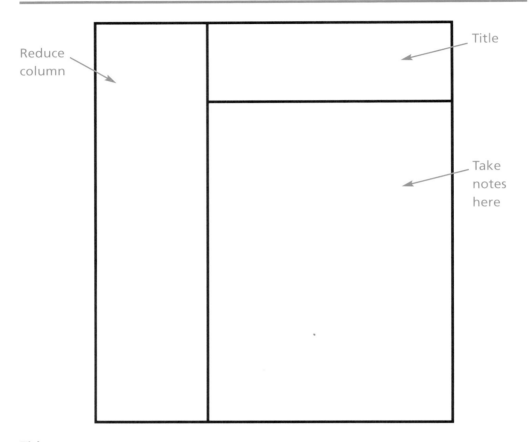

Title

Always put a title on your notes; it helps when you need to organise them later. In this title put the subject, topic and date of the notes. If you are taking notes from a textbook, add in the name of the chapter you concentrated on.

Reduce column

A **reduce column** is a space you leave to one side of the page for use at a later time. When you come back to review your notes you can use the reduce column to add in prompting questions, key words or learning techniques.

Leave space

When you take notes into the section of the page you have left for this purpose, make sure you leave lots of space. Skip a few lines after paragraphs or after a particular list of points. You will need to use this space for adding in any extra information you might want to add when you are reviewing and learning your notes.

Methods of note taking

There are many different ways of taking notes. It's usually a good idea to use a few different types of note-taking methods to vary things and keep your work interesting and easy to remember. I outline the main ones below to help you find those which suit you or the topic you are revising best.

Linear method

The linear method of note taking means that you organise your notes with a heading and list of bulleted points or numbered points. These notes about the advantages of taking notes are organised in the linear method.

Table 8.1: Advantages of taking notes (linear method)

For homework/study:	For exam revision:
• Aids understanding.	• Information already organised for easy reference.
• Helps planning of essays/answers.	• Easier to learn key words and phrases.
• Work is reduced to important information.	• Notes are more memorable visually.
• Information is organised for learning.	• Manageable amount of material for
last-minute recaps.	

Spider-diagram method

The spider-diagram method means that you write the title of your notes in the **middle of the page** and then spread your notes around this title. These can be very good for any student who likes to learn with visual aids. The notes in Figure 8.2 on bad habits of note taking are written in the spider-diagram method.

Figure 8.2: Bad habits of note taking (Spider-diagram method)

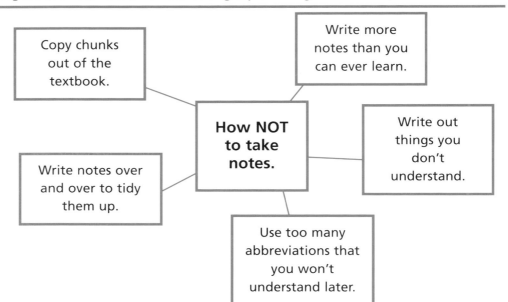

Venn-diagram method

In this method you can cross-reference information that overlaps from one topic to another (that is, when two topics have the same information in common).

These notes on strategies for note taking and tidying notes shows the Venn-diagram system at work.

Figure 8.3: Strategies for note taking/tidying messy notes (Venn-diagram method)

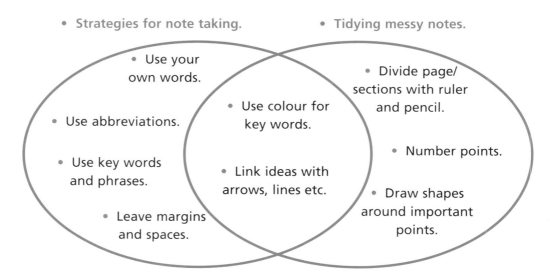

Alternative methods for note taking

Another interesting method of taking notes is to write them up in a visual way that will help you remember them. Two such examples would be to use a tree or river to write notes in an eye-catching way.

When you take notes using a tree as your basic structure, each main branch becomes a section heading, with smaller branches becoming sub-sections of that main section. In the same way, a river is one section, while estuaries are sub-headings you need to learn within that main topic. Here is an example to show you how you might represent listening skills with a tree method:

Figure 8.4: Listening skills (Alternative methods for note taking)

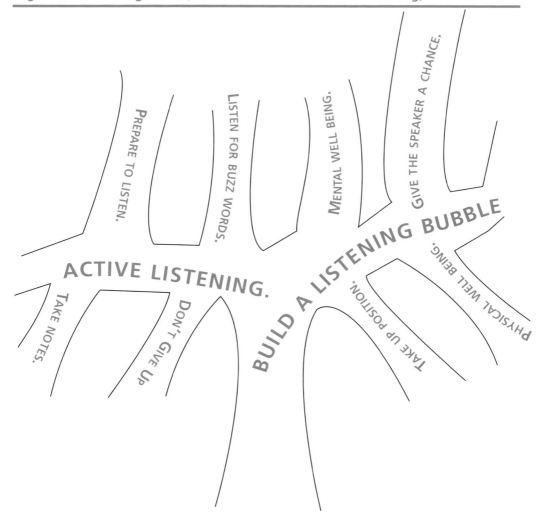

How to take notes in class

Many of the notes you take will be in class. Quite often, the teacher will give you those notes, either on a handout, as an overhead or as dictation. However, if you need to take notes just from listening to the teacher then you need to follow some guidelines.

Prepare your notes page

Make sure you have your notes page ready for note taking (see 'Organising the page for note taking' on page 54). Leave a reduce column for use later and put your title on the top. In this title include the topic you are studying and the date of the class – this will distinguish these notes from any you might take from a textbook.

Don't try to take everything down

You can't write as fast as someone talks, so you need to keep in mind that you can only take down a certain amount of information. You need to listen out for what you think are the most important points.

To help decide what's important, listen for 'buzz words', key phrases like: 'To sum up', 'The three main reasons are … ', 'In conclusion', 'To review', 'This is important', 'Remember that … ', 'Keep in mind' etc. Phrases like these always lead into key points so that's the time to take notes.

Leave lots of space

It's always a good idea to leave lots of space around and under your notes. You can leave a few lines after each paragraph. This will be useful later if you want to add to your own points or clarify anything.

How to take notes from a textbook

You may find it intimidating to face learning an entire chapter of your textbook. The best way to approach a task like this is to *take notes* from that chapter. Then your main concern is to reduce the chapter down to the most important ideas you need to learn. I outline the best way method for doing this below.

Skim the chapter

First read quickly through the chapter introduction, section headings, anything in *italics*, **bold text** and bulleted points and the chapter summary. This will show you what the chapter is about and the section headings tell you the most important topics in the chapter. You have now already prepared yourself to learn certain important areas.

Prepare your notes page

Get your notes page ready (see page 54, 'Organising the page for note taking') with a reduce column and put your title on the top. In the title include the topic you are studying and the chapter number – this distinguishes these notes from any you might take in class on the same topic.

Ask questions

The best way to take notes in this situation is to ask yourself questions to which you find the answers. There are two advantages of this question-and-answer format.

First, when you ask yourself a question and read to find the answer, you will be able to concentrate better on reading.

Second, it will be easier to learn these notes in a question-and-answer format. This will help you also if you study with friends or want some family member to help. They can test your knowledge by asking you the questions you have already laid out. Alternatively, you can test your own knowledge by hiding the notes and reading through and answering the questions in the left column.

The easiest way to come up with questions is to turn each section heading into a question. For example, if a section heading in a Geography chapter on 'Mass

Movement' is 'Mechanical Weathering', your question here can be 'What is mechanical weathering?'

Write this question in your reduce column and then read the appropriate section to find the answer. Try to reduce the answer to the absolute minimum explanation – you only want to have to learn as much as you need to, so whatever you do, avoid rewriting the whole paragraph.

Continue your questioning format all the way through the chapter, making sure you ask questions relating to the section headings and the important bulleted points, italics and bold text.

Put the notes in your own words

It's important that you put the notes into *your own words*. Not only is it easier to learn your own words than someone else's, but if you do put the notes in your own words it means that you will have to understand the material you are working with. Clearly then, this is an excellent start to learning it.

Use lists and bullets

As you take the notes, try to use numbered points and bulleted points to break information down to key words and phrases. Remember, you are looking for the important *facts* that you need to learn. You might also use coloured pens and highlighter to make some information stand out as particularly important.

How to arrange notes for learning

Frequently, when you take notes in class, they are still quite long-winded and disorganised. It's a good idea then to arrange those notes in a more organised way for learning. At this stage many students will rewrite the notes again but there is actually no need to do that. That's an inefficient way to use your time. Instead, you just need to arrange them in a way that makes it easier to pick out the facts you need to learn. I explain how to do this now.

Review notes quickly

First and foremost, it is essential that you read back over your notes as soon after you have taken them down as possible – that night is the best option but at least that weekend. In this way, they are still fresh in your mind and it is easier to be clear about what you *meant* to take down.

One quick read

Take one quick read through all the notes you took in that one class. This gives you an overall impression of the whole topic.

Reduce each section

Take each section or paragraph in turn and use your reduce column to ask yourself questions relating to the main points of your notes. For example, if your History notes tell you that 'the Celts originally came from an area in central Europe around Southern Germany and Austria', the question you could ask here is 'Where did the Celts come from?' This question goes into your reduce column and then you take your highlighter and highlight the answer, 'central Europe around Germany and Austria.'

You can also use your reduce column to write key words and phrases that you must learn. For example, if your History notes are about the training of a knight in Medieval times, you might want to put the three main stages in your reduce column: 'Page, age 7; Squire, age 14; Knight, age 21'.

Add in any explanations you need

Quite often, after you take notes and then go back and read them, you may find that there is something that doesn't make sense or something that you thought you'd remember that you don't now. Use the space you left after each paragraph to add in any explanations of terms you don't understand or other points you think are important.

Once you've completed this tidying-up process, your notes are more manageable. You can now learn in the question-and-answer format and key concepts are highlighted or are in your reduce column.

Sample notes

Here is a fairly typical example of notes you might take in History class. They are about the Celtic people in ancient Ireland.

Figure 8.5: Handwritten Celts Notes 1

Celtic Ireland. Introduction to the Celts. Lesson 1. 6/11/07

Archaeologists continue to discover new evidence about Irish society in ancient times and this helps historians piece together information about life for the Celtic people in Ireland. The Celts came to Ireland in 300 BC and archaeologists have discovered many artefacts that give us lots of insights into how they lived. The Celts originally came from an area in central Europe around Southern Germany and Austria. They spoke their own language and developed a Celtic culture that historians are still learning about.

They lived in homes called ringforts and hillforts. These were made of wattle and daub and had thatched roofs. They were made up of large circular enclosures with all the buildings inside the enclosure. They would also bring animals into this enclosure at night. The hillforts were built on high ground.

The Celts used weapons made of iron and they were farmers, working the land, rearing cattle and growing vegetables. Evidence from discoveries has helped us piece these details together.

Celtic society was organised as follows: King; Nobles (warriors, had land and cattle); Aos Dana (learned people, special skills, highly respected); Farmers (worked land of nobles); Slaves (captured in war, did most of work, no pay)

Figure 8.6: Handwritten Celts Notes 2

Celtic Ireland. Introduction to the Celts. Lesson 1. 6/11/07

When did Celts come to Ireland?

Where did Celts come from?

What weapons?
Living?

King
Nobles
Aos Dana
Farmers
Slaves

Archaeologists continue to discover new evidence about Irish society in ancient times and this helps historians piece together information about life for the Celtic people in Ireland. The Celts came to Ireland in 300 BC and archaeologists have discovered many artefacts that give us lots of insights into how they lived. The Celts originally came from an area in central Europe around Southern Germany and Austria. They spoke their own language and developed a Celtic culture that historians are still learning about.

They lived in homes called ringforts and hillforts. These were made of wattle and daub and had thatched roofs. They were made up of large circular enclosures with all the buildings inside the enclosure. They would also bring animals into this enclosure at night. The hillforts were built on high ground.

The Celts used weapons made of iron and they were farmers, working the land, rearing cattle and growing vegetables. Evidence from discoveries has helped us piece these details together.

Celtic society was organised as follows: King; Nobles (warriors, had land and cattle); Aos Dana (learned people, special skills, highly respected); Farmers (worked land of nobles); Slaves (captured in war, did most of work, no pay)

Tidying up these notes for learning

From this example, you can see that when you review your notes after class you can use your reduce column to make key words stand out, draw pictures to help you remember things and for questions. You then highlight the answers to these questions.

Now you just need to learn the questions and the answers you have highlighted and any other notes that have been added to the reduce column or brought to your attention by boxes or circles or pictures.

Note that you can reduce these notes quite significantly. Weed out any extra information that you don't need to learn, like the introductory sentence: 'Archaeologists continue to discover new evidence about Irish society in ancient times and this helps historians piece together information about life for the Celtic people in Ireland.' This is just an introduction to the paragraph and you could easily write one of those in an exam, so there's no need to learn that.

What you should concentrate on is picking out and learning the *facts* about Celtic Ireland, which begins with the fact that they came to Ireland in 300 BC.

Always tidy up your notes in this way as soon after the lesson as you can, while they are still fresh in your mind.

A quick guide to keeping your notes organised

- Write your notes on hole-punched A4 paper or cue cards for easy filing.
- Divide notes into folders for each subject, using dividers for each topic or, in the case of cue cards, in a small box with dividers.
- Title and number pages for easy filing.
- Use a reduce column for questions and key words and phrases.
- Use highlighters, different coloured pens, boxes and circles to bring attention to very important information.
- File notes as quickly as possible after you write them. You don't want to lose them!
- Review your notes regularly. This means that you need to keep reading back over notes and learn them many times over.

9 Memory tricks

What are memory tricks? Memory tricks are strategies you can use to help hold information in long-term memory and then access it when you need it.

After an exam students will often say, 'My mind went blank, I couldn't remember anything!'

Well, thankfully there is no such thing as a blank mind but what they mean is that they couldn't *access* the information they needed.

How memory works: short-term and long-term memory

Your brain is a complex organ, but if you think of it in simple terms, you have a **short-term** memory and a **long-term** memory. When you learn something once, you store it in your short-term memory. For example, you might repeat a phone number to yourself a few times in order to remember it for as long as it takes you to get to the phone and dial it. However, if you wanted to remember that number in a week or month's time, you would have to put it into your long-term memory.

In relation to exams then, once something has been learned enough to stay in your long-term memory, you want to be able to access that information when you need it. This is where memory tricks come in.

General memory strategies

Repetition, repetition, repetition

The best way to remember something is to keep repeating the information. Recite the material to yourself or write it out over and over. Learn the original then try to repeat it without looking back. When you have completed all of it that you can remember, check back against the original and fill in what you missed. Learn again and then go back over the repetition process. Continue to do this until you feel comfortable that you have learned it well. Come back to it a day or two later and repeat the whole process again. Soon you will be able to repeat it without looking back at all and then you will know it's stored in your brain.

Review notes quickly

When you take notes in class or from a textbook, you've already begun the learning process. Don't lose that momentum by putting aside those notes and forgetting about them. Read back over them as quickly as you can, preferably that night, or at least that weekend. In this way they will still be fresh in your mind and it will be easier to learn them. (See Chapter 8 above for note-taking skills.)

Another advantage of a quick review is the fact that you can spot immediately what doesn't make sense and remedy it by checking against your textbook or earlier notes. If you still can't understand exactly what you took down, go back and ask your teacher the next day.

Review notes regularly

In the introduction to this book you were reminded that when you learn things only once, you soon forget a large chunk of them. So it is essential to keep going over notes. Review them regularly. When you take down notes, review them as soon as possible afterwards and then the next week again. Each month go back over notes again. In this way you continue to keep them fresh in your mind and are committing them even more solidly to memory.

Reduce notes

Like many students, you would probably like to cut the amount of material you must have to learn to a minimum. Chapter 8 shows how you can do this by **reducing** your notes to key words and phrases. Look out for the actual *facts* that you have to learn and highlight those. When you get to the exam, you can take those key facts and expand them into an answer.

Language memory skills

Use CDs

When you are learning a language, the best way to do it is to listen to as much of that language as possible. Listen to language CDs and try to repeat each phrase as you hear it. Alternatively, tape yourself speaking the language or reading out a passage and listen back to it, repeating as you go along. The language CDs with past exam papers are particularly beneficial.

For more ideas on learning for an aural exam, see Chapter 19, 'Preparing for aural exams'.

Set aside language time

Another essential to learning a language is to speak it as often as possible. Aim to speak in the language you're learning for at least ten minutes every day. Allocate a time when you will attempt to speak the language and try to put everything you want to say in that time into say, French. Alternatively meet up with one of your friends and speak that language to each other for a set amount of time.

For more ideas on learning for an oral exam, see Chapter 18, 'Preparing for oral exams'.

Memory tricks

Memory tricks are more defined shortcuts to storing information in your brain for ease of access.

Acronyms

Using acronyms means that you take the first letter of each word in a list of words or phrases you have to learn and form a word or words with them that you will remember easily. When you need to recall the information you write out your word(s) and then fill in the list.

Take for example this set of phrases from Business Studies.

Here you need to learn the factors a business has to take into consideration when choosing a source of finance. They are:

1 Purpose for which they need the money.
2 Time the money is needed for.
3 Cost of the finance.
4 Tax implications.
5 Repayments required.
6 Eligibility for government grants.
7 Security required.
8 The different options (short term, medium term, long term).

In order to learn this list, the first step to take is to pick out and highlight the key word in each point, like this:

1 **Purpose** for which they need the money.
2 **Time** the money is needed for.
3 **Cost** of the finance.

4   **Tax** implications.
5   **Repayments.**
6   **Eligibility** for government grants.
7   **Security** required.
8   The different **options** (short term, medium term, long term).

Now take the first letter of each of these key words:

   P, T, C, T, R, E, S, O

Shuffle the letters around to spell a word or more than one word.

   For example: CREST TOP

Now take a coloured pen and write out your chosen word vertically down a page
like this:

   C

   R

   E

   S

   T

   T

   O

   P

Next take a different colour pen and fill in the rest of the word or phrase as you
need to learn it:

1   Cost of the finance.
2   Repayments.
3   Eligibility for government grants.
4   Security required.
5   Time money is needed for.
6   Tax implications.
7   Options (short term, medium term and long term).
8   Purpose for which they need the money.

Learn your list this way by repeating it to yourself. Work slowly through the list
saying each phrase clearly as you go. Then cover it and write CREST TOP down
your page again. Try to fill in all the ones you remember.

If you miss some, look back at your original list and fill those in, repeating them as you go. Once again write them out without looking back. Repeat this process a few times until you can write the full list without missing any.

Come back the next day and try to write them out again. Relearn any you missed and continue to review them occasionally when you have a few free minutes at the end of study time.

When you get to the exam and you are asked about the factors a business takes into consideration when choosing a source of finance, you can recall the information by realising that you learned the list using CREST TOP. Write out your list and expand your answer from there.

Acrostics

Using acrostics is similar to using acronyms. However, here you take the first letter of the words you want to learn but instead of forming a word or words to remember, you form a **sentence** or **phrase**.

Say you had to learn this list of stakeholders in a business:

Suppliers, consumers, entrepreneurs, government, society, managers, owners, workers.

Your first step is to highlight each of the first letters of the elements of this list. Here you would write:

S, C, E, G, S, M, O, W

If you shuffle these around, you can form a sentence like this:

Silly **s**entences **c**ome to **m**ind **w**hen **g**oing **o**ver **e**xams.

Now when you want to learn the stakeholders in a business, you write out your sentence, take each of the first letters highlighted and fill in each stakeholder. Learn this list and then try to write them out without looking back. Check your answer and fill in any you might have missed. Repeat this process until you feel comfortable writing them out without looking back.

When you get to the exam and you are asked for the stakeholders in a business you will remember that you learned this with your sentence, 'Silly sentences come to mind when going over exams.' You write out your sentence, fill in your list with the help of the first letters and take your answer from there.

A good tip to keep in mind when using this method is to make your sentences as silly (or as rude) as possible. The sillier they are the easier it is to remember them!

Rhyme

None of us ever forgets nursery rhymes from childhood like 'Humpty Dumpty', partly because they were repeated to us so many times but mostly because the rhyme was easy to learn. Rhyme gave them a rhythm and song effect that is easy to retain in our memories.

It can be useful, therefore, to use rhyme in learning. For instance, if you are having difficulty learning a piece of information, then you might want to incorporate it into a rhyme that you can learn off.

In this example I use a table taken from Home Economics to show how you can use rhyme to learn the composition of meat.

Table 9.1: Rhyming: composition of meat					
Fat	Protein	Water	Vitamins	Minerals	Carbohydrates
21	24	54	A, B1, B2, Niacin	0.7	0

Often it can be difficult to remember percentages like this and it's very easy to get them mixed up. By putting them into a short rhyme, you can keep them clear in your mind:

> 24 protein and 21 fats
> 0 carbohydrate and vitamins, the brats,
> Niacin B1, B2, and vitamin A
> 54 water, .7 min OK

By repeating this rhyme many times you should be able to keep it in your memory and recite it in the exam and then build your answer from there.

Write, read, cover, write, review

This method is particularly good for learning vocabulary. Draw out a table like this one below with about six columns.

Table 9.2: French vocabulary				
Mon père				
Ma mère				
Ma famille				
Ma soeur				
Mon frère				

1   Fill in the words you need to learn in the first column (in this example I am using some French words related to the family).
2   Take some time to read them and learn the spelling.
3   Cover that first column and try to write them out without looking back in the second column.
4   Correct, or review, what you have done and relearn them.
5   Cover the first two columns and write the list into the third column and correct again.
6   Repeat this process for all the columns.
7   When you reach the last one you should be able to write them out without any errors.

When you use this method it is a good idea to learn a small group of words at a time, rather than trying to learn a long list. If you have a long list to learn, break it into groups of between five and ten words and don't move onto the next group until you have mastered the previous one.

Use pictures

If you were asked to look at this list of household appliances you might have to learn for Home Economics, which words do you think would stick immediately in your mind?

- kettle
- coffee maker
- deep-fat fryer
- electric frying pan
- mixer
- food processor
- carving knife
- iron

- liquidiser
- refrigerator
- washing machine
- toaster.

Probably the ones that would easily stick in your mind would be kettle, iron and toaster. Why? Because of the pictures. The pictures make the words stand out and help you visualise the words. Later when you try to recall the list you will see clearly in your mind the kettle, iron and toaster.

Use a picture layout

It can be also be helpful to put the information you need to learn into a picture. This will help organise the information and you'll be able to visualise it when you need to recall it in the exam.

Imagine you need to learn the layout for writing a review for your English exam. When you write a review you know you want to divide it into certain paragraphs and those paragraphs need to be written in a certain order that you need to learn. Your first paragraph will be details like author name, publisher etc. for a book; the second paragraph will be your introduction; the third is the plot outline; the fourth is your own opinion; and the last paragraph is your recommendation.

If you incorporate this information into a picture, it might look something like this:

Figure 9.4: How to write a Review/Car Illustration

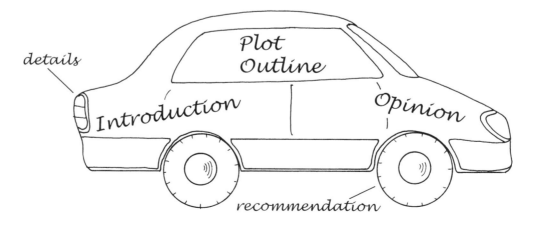

Take this picture, stick it up on your wall over your study desk and study it regularly until you can picture all the elements without checking back to the original.

Now, in the exam, if you are asked to write a review you will be able to picture in your mind the car and in this way recall the outline you need to follow.

Use visualisation

You have seen how effective pictures can be in learning. Following on from that, it is often a good idea to visualise yourself doing something and placing the things you have to learn as you go. Later when you are in the exam you visualise yourself doing that thing again and you pick up the things you needed to learn on the way.

Let's take as an example a list of poems by Robert Frost that you might need to remember for your English exam.

- 'The Road Not Taken'
- 'Out, Out –'
- 'After Apple-Picking'
- 'The Tuft of Flowers'
- 'Mending Wall'
- 'Birches'
- 'Spring Pools'
- 'Acquainted With Night'

Take key words from the titles that will jog your memory of each poem and now imagine yourself doing something ordinary like walking into and around a garden or park.

> So I'm walking up to the gates of the park but they're closed with a sign saying **'Out, Out'**. I glance around and climb one of the **Birches** to get over the high **wall**, which, by the way, needs **mending**. It's pitch dark at **night** here and I can barely see the **road** ahead, which looks grassy and not travelled much. I trip and fall into a **tuft of flowers** and break them. I hear a noise behind, look over a hedge and see young boys **picking apples**. As they run away with the apples they fall into two **pools** that have strange **spring**-like sculptures around the sides. Serves them right!

Now take this visualisation and go over it in your mind many times. Once again when you are in the exam and need to recall these poems relating to Frost, you can simply picture your trip into and around the park and pick up the key items you need.

It's a good idea to have a list of locations you can use when you need to visualise something you want to learn. Here I've used a park but you can have a store of locations like your house, your home town, the shopping centre and so on. When you want to learn a range of ideas, picture yourself walking around these places and put the ideas you want to learn in different locations.

It is also a good idea to make the images you form in your mind as silly, rude or outrageous as you can imagine. This makes it a lot easier to learn.

Use stories

In this variation on visualisation, you make up a story in which you put in the phrases or words you need to learn.

For instance, this story could help you learn a few important artists and their works for your History exam:

> Amy went to the most unusual Christmas party last year. Firstly you had to pay on the way in and when you did you were called a **patron**. On the walls there were lots of **frescoes** painted of **nudes**, **human anatomy** and **landscapes**. In one corner there was actually a wedding taking place, which my host told me was **The Arnolfini Wedding**, although the groom's name was **Van Eyck**. Sitting at one table was a woman called **Mona Lisa** (she had the most unusual smile). She was reading *The **da Vinci** Code* and was eating what she said was her **Last Supper**. There was an Italian guy there called **Donatello** who was sitting on the floor drinking wine and leaning against a statue called **David**. Another Italian came up to me and said he had just come from the **Sistine Chapel** and could definitely give a **Last Judgement** that this was a most unusual party.

By repeating this story and committing it to memory, it will be easy to recall key words in the History exam.

Use flash cards

Flash cards (also called cue cards) are small lined cards. To use them effectively, write a short key phrase or idea on each one and use these to aid your learning.

Probably the best way to use flash cards is to:

1   Write a question on one side and the answer on the other side.
2   Divide them into topics within each subject.
3   Choose one topic per study session and go over your flash cards, reading the question and then attempting to answer it without looking at the back.
4   Correct your answer and relearn.
5   Repeat the process until you have answered all the questions easily.

Use diagrams and flow charts

Often it is easier to learn a diagram than to learn a few paragraphs of writing. Use diagrams and flow charts whenever you can. You will find them particularly useful in subjects like Geography and the Science subjects. Practise drawing the diagram and filling in the elements; use lots of colour for different sections.

It can also be useful to draw out the diagram or flow chart, cut it up into sections and then piece them back together in the correct order like a jigsaw.

Use underlines and other visual aids

In your notes use underlines, boxes and circles to make key words stand out. You can also use capital letters and coloured pens and highlighters. This draws attention to ideas and makes them easier to remember.

Link ideas

Use a colour-coded system to link ideas. For example, on page 1 of your notes you may have some notes on Hitler that you need to learn. Later, on page 5 you have some more. In this case, **colour code** all your notes relating to Hitler in say green (either by writing with green pen, underlining in green or highlighting in green). This means that you will be able to find all your Hitler notes easily and it can also help your recall by thinking about all the ideas you had in green.

Group concepts

Take a look at these two lists and decide which list you think would be easier to learn.

List 1

- kitchen
- apple
- student
- bedroom
- orange
- teacher
- harp
- principal
- bathroom
- dog
- chair

- accordion
- hall
- guitar
- pear
- classroom

List 2

House	Fruit	School	Music
Kitchen	Pear	Classroom	Harp
Bedroom	Apple	Principal	Accordion
Hall	Orange	Teacher	Guitar
Bathroom	Banana	Student	Drums

Most people would find List 2 easier to learn. Why? Because it is organised into groups, which makes it easier to remember.

Therefore, in your own learning it is a good idea to keep your work organised and to group different concepts under topic headings. For example, in History when you learn about the Renaissance, you could group inventions and advancements under headings like: Medicine, Art, Science, Writing, Printing.

How to learn a text off by heart

Write it out!

Many of the tricks so far have been useful for learning key words and phrases. But what happens when you want to learn an essay, for instance, off by heart, which many students do?

In this case the best thing to do is write out the essay several times until you feel comfortable with what you want to say. However, recalling the whole thing in an exam can then be difficult. For this you need to break it down to something a little more manageable.

Use the subject lines

Take the subject line of each paragraph and learn those using a memory trick of your choice. Every paragraph has a subject line, which contains the main point of the paragraph. Once you can remember this main point, you can easily build your paragraph around it.

Learn the first line

Alternatively, you could learn the first line of each paragraph. Once you have the first line to launch you into the paragraph, the rest comes more easily.

Use the reduce column

Another good method to use is to make use of a reduce column again. Put key concepts from each paragraph into the reduce column and learn those; again you can then build your paragraph around those.

Use pictures

Lastly, try drawing little pictures into the reduce column and this will help aid recall. For example, if your paragraph was about a day at the beach, draw a beach into your reduce column which will help it stick in your mind.

Some quick tips for using memory tricks

- Use a wide range of memory tricks so that you don't become too dependent on just one.
- Use a memory trick when you are having particular difficulty with learning something.
- Practise each one and then choose the ones that suit you best.
- Jot the memory trick into the reduce column of your notes to aid learning each time you review your notes.

Section 4

Writing Skills that Impress

The importance of good writing skills cannot be overemphasised. Most of the examinations throughout your school career will be written ones, so an ability to write effectively is a must have. Good writing means good spelling; excellent grammar and punctuation; clear and logical sentence structuring; clear and sensible paragraphing and the use of a wide vocabulary. If your writing has all these key elements, then it will be easy to read and understand, and you will impress not only the casual reader but also, more importantly, the examiner.

What you will learn in Section 4

In this section you will learn everything you need to know about:
- spelling
- grammar and punctuation
- sentence structuring
- paragraphing
- widening your vocabulary.

10 Improving your spelling

We all spell words incorrectly at times. That's not the problem here. What *is* a problem is misspelling the same word over and over again. There is no excuse for it. With some simple methods that I outline below, you can work on reducing your spelling errors and aim towards better writing skills.

Form good spelling habits

Let's face it, the main reason many of us don't pay attention to our spelling is that we can't be bothered. You may want to get your homework done quickly and you don't want to waste time. It may seem easier (and quicker) to just leave it to the teacher to correct any misspelling.

But if you learn to take care when you're writing and get into the habit of correcting your own spelling, you will become a more effective writer.

Just take a little time and care and you'll be able to correct many of your own errors. Simply taking the time to think about which version of 'its' you need ('its' or 'it's'?) or which 'there' you need ('there', 'they're' or 'their') can save many mistakes.

Use your mistakes to learn

The most important thing you can do to improve your spelling is to *learn from your mistakes.* When the teacher corrects your spelling, take three of those corrected words and learn the right spelling. If you do this, you won't be trying to learn too many words at the same time. (It is generally easier to learn in groups of three.)

Write, learn, cover and review

You can do this by using the ever-popular **write**, **learn**, **cover** and **review** method:

- Write the word out correctly.
- Learn it.
- Cover it.

- Write it out again.
- Correct your second one against the right spelling.

Continue the process until you feel comfortable that you know the word. Do this for the three words you have decided to learn today.

Make sure that you keep these lists of words you have misspelled in the past for easy reference until you are completely sure that you will always get them right.

Learn by syllable

If you are having difficulty spelling longer words, it can be a good idea to break them into syllables and learn them that way.

For example:

- dictionary: dic-tion-ary
- extraordinary: ex-tra-or-din-ary
- escalate: es-ca-late

Work with a dictionary

People often spell words wrongly because they guess the word and don't bother to check if they are right. Always use a **dictionary** when you are unsure of a spelling. If you do this, you will get it right from the beginning and you won't get into the habit of spelling it your way instead of how it should be spelled.

Learn from other writers

When you read a book, magazine or newspaper, pay careful attention to the words. If you come across a word you weren't sure how to spell, highlight it or take it down and learn to spell it correctly.

Learn from word processing

When you type in a word-processing program like Microsoft Word, the software will automatically put a red line under any words you misspell. Take note of the words you frequently get red lines under and learn the correct spelling. Keep a notepad beside you for this purpose.

Divide each page into two columns, one titled 'Wrong' the other titled 'Correct' and write down how you spelled the word incorrectly in the 'Wrong' column and then write the correct way in the 'Correct' column. This way you'll see a pattern emerging of the common spelling errors you tend to make and you can work towards improving these. It also means you have a handy list of words you should learn. However, do make sure that your Word is set to 'UK English' rather than 'US English' or it may pick up words that are simply spelled differently in the United States.

Basic spelling rules

There are some accepted **rules** when it comes to spelling. It's a good idea to learn these off by heart. That way you can avoid any silly errors regarding things like 'i' and 'e' use and doubling final consonants.

Here are the main rules you will find useful:

'I' before 'e' except after 'c'.

This means that when you have a word with an 'i' and 'e' coming together, you must put the 'i' before the 'e', unless they come after a 'c'.

For example, when there is no 'c':

- believe
- thief
- fierce
- friend

But after a 'c':

- receive
- conceive
- deceive
- ceiling

When you add the prefixes, 'mis-', 'il-', 'in-', 'dis-', 're-', 'over-' to a word, the spelling of that word remains the same.

For example:

- Mis + demeanour = misdemeanour
- Il + legitimate = illegitimate
- In + edible = inedible
- Dis + satisfied = dissatisfied
- Re + run = rerun
- Over + come = overcome

When a word ends in the letter 'y', change the 'y' to 'i' when you add any suffix like '-ly', '-ment', '-ness-', '-ful'.

For example:

- body: bodily
- merry: merriment
- happy: happiness
- duty: dutiful

If a word ends in 'e' and you want to add a suffix that begins with a vowel, like '-ing', '-able', '-ity', '-ous', drop the 'e'.

For example:

- argue: arguing
- like: likable
- obese: obesity
- desire: desirous

When you add a suffix like '-ed', '-ance', '-ing', '-ent', double the final consonant when it is a one-syllable word or the final accent is on the last syllable. You also double the consonant when the word ends in a single vowel and a single consonant.

For example:

- hop: hopped
- commit: committing
- occur: occurred

- allot: allotting
- concur: concurrent
- remit: remittance

When making a word plural, you usually add '-s'.

For example:

- employee: employees
- plural: plurals
- cat: cats

When a word ends in 's', 'x', 'z', 'ch', 'sh', add '-es' to make it plural.

For example:

- bush: bushes
- business: businesses
- tax: taxes
- catch: catches

When a word ends in 'y' and is preceded by a consonant, change the 'y' to 'i' and add '-es'.

For example:

- company: companies
- lottery: lotteries

When a word ends in 'y' but is preceded by a vowel, just add '-s'.

For example:

- monkey: monkeys
- key: keys

Words ending in 'o' generally are made plural by adding '-s'.

For example:

- studio: studios
- radio: radios

However, when that 'o' is preceded by a consonant, you must add '-es' to make it plural.

For example:

- potato: potatoes
- hero: heroes

When words end in 'f' or 'fe', you must change the 'f' to 'v'; and add '-s' to make it plural.

For example:

- knife: knives
- wife: wives
- life: lives
- shelf: shelves

The plurals of some words don't follow any of these rules and are different forms of the word. So you must learn them as you come across them.

For example:

- mouse: mice
- child: children
- man: men

Remember, some words are the same in singular and plural.

For example:

- sheep: sheep
- deer: deer

Spot commonly misspelled words

There are many words that all of us have difficulty spelling, maybe because they don't spell the way they sound or they go against the accepted rules of spelling. Here is a list of words that most people have problems spelling. By learning this list you can avoid these same mistakes.

Table 10.1 Commonly misspelled words

Absence	Exaggerate	Medicine	Rhythm
Accommodate	Excellent	Minutes	Ridiculous
Achieve	Excitement	Mischief	Scene
Agreeable	Existence	Necessary	Science
Amateur	Extremely	Negotiate	Sense
Appearance	February	Niece	Sentence
Awkward	Foreigner	Occasionally	Separate
Awful	Friend	Organiser	Similar
Beautiful	Fulfil	Panic	Sincerely
Beginning	Grievance	Parallel	Skilful
Breathe	Government	Paralysis	Soliloquy
Business	Guarantee	Parliament	Surprise
Cemetery	Guard	Permanent	Taught
Changeable	Height	Personnel	Thorough
Clothes	Humorous	Physical	Thought
College	Hypocrisy	Poem	Through
Commitment	Immediately	Poetry	Tragedy
Committee	Immigrate	Possesses	Truly
Conscience	Independence	Privilege	Twelfth
Courageous	Intelligence	Psychology	Unconscious
Courtesy	Irresistible	Pursue	Unnecessary
Definitely	Know	Queue	Until
Develop	Knowledge	Quiet	Usual
Disappointment	Leisure	Quite	Usually
Does	Liaison	Receipt	Vicious
Dying	Loneliness	Receive	Wednesday
Eight	Lose	Recognise	Weight
Embarrassed	Maintain	Recommend	Whole
Emigrate	Maintenance	Repetition	Weird
Enthusiasm	Marriage	Restaurant	Woollen
Essential	Mechanic	Rhyme	

Learn to distinguish between 'proper' English and 'texting' English

Because we text so often in our daily lives, we have become used to abbreviating words and spelling them in simplified ways, to save space in our messages. It is then very easy to get so used to this spelling that we put it into our school essays and tests.

Stay aware of this and be careful to read back over your written work to pick out where you might have used 'texting' language. Words like 'fone' instead of 'phone' and 'skol' instead of 'school' are just two examples of what to look out for.

11 Improving your grammar and punctuation

You may think of grammar as boring, but good grammar is essential for good writing. Without clear grammar and punctuation, readers would not be able to understand the writer's intentions. Grammar and punctuation give order and logic to your writing and they are vital if you want to write well.

Learn from your mistakes

Once again, one of the best ways to learn good grammar and punctuation is to learn from your mistakes. Pay attention to any corrections your teacher makes to your work, and practise the sentence with their correction. Then practise similar sentences to reinforce what you have learned.

If you are in any doubt as to *why* the teacher has corrected a verb tense or a comma, then just ask. The more you learn to question how grammar works and the way it works, the more competent you will become at using it correctly.

Learn the rules of punctuation

Most often, the mistakes we make when writing are based around the incorrect use of punctuation marks like commas, apostrophes and full stops. So, learning the rules of punctuation, or referring to them when in doubt, can improve your writing immensely.

Here are the main punctuation rules to keep in mind:

The full stop (.)

- Use full stops at the end of sentences. *Always* finish a sentence with a full stop.
- Full stops can also be used for abbreviations like Co. (county) and e.g. (for example) but not usually when the abbreviation is made up of the first letters of the organisation like RTE, ESB.

The comma (,)

■ Use commas when listing items. For example:

 I went to the shop and bought jeans, a sweatshirt, T-shirt and runners.

(Note that you don't need to use the comma before the last item.)

■ Use a comma to separate a clause in a sentence that is used to explain the subject. For example:

 The student, who had won an award at the science fair, aced his exams.

■ Use a comma to separate text from direct speech. For example:

 My teacher said, 'We all have to learn grammar, whether we like it or not.'

■ Use commas to separate the person addressed from the speech. For example:

 'Ms Collins, please be kind when you correct my essay!'

■ Use commas to separate out the different parts of an address. For example:

 1 Berkley Court, Manchester Rd, London.

The inverted comma (')

■ Use inverted commas for direct speech (i.e. writing what someone says). For example:

 Bart says, 'Eat my shorts!'

■ Use inverted commas when you quote from a piece of writing. For example:

 Wordsworth begins his poem with the simile, 'I wandered lonely as a cloud.'

■ Use inverted commas for the titles of phrases, songs, chapters and poems. For example:

 One of my favourite songs is Bob Marley's 'Redemption song'.

The apostrophe (')

■ Use apostrophes to show possession. For example:

 Tammy's song went to number one in the charts.
 Shane's anger boiled over.
 All the babies' bibs were soiled.
 I like to read Yeats's poems.

■ Use apostrophes to show missing letters after you put two words together. For example:

> I have: I've
> It is: It's
> They will: They'll
> The '92 final

■ Use apostrophes to indicate time or quantity. For example:
> One month's time.

The question mark (?) and exclamation mark (!)

■ Use a question mark at the end of a question. For example:

> Do you find punctuation lessons exciting?

■ Use an exclamation mark to convey surprise or shock or raised voices. For example:

> 'Stop thief!' the guard yelled.

The colon (:) and semi-colon (;)

■ Use a colon to introduce a list of items. For example:

> We use four ingredients in this recipe: flour, sugar, milk and eggs.

■ Use a semi-colon to link two separate clauses into one sentence. For example:

> No need to send any money now; we will send you a bill later.

■ You can use a semi-colon when you write a list if each element of the list is a long phrase or if a comma separates some individually. For example:

> To win the competition you need to be able to sing well; play an instrument; have a talent like juggling, fire eating or gymnastics; or show that you are a magician.

The dash (–) and hyphen (-)

The best way to distinguish between a dash and a hyphen is to remember that a dash (—) is slightly longer than the hyphen (-).

■ Use dashes to separate an aside from the rest of the sentence. For example:

> This book – in case you are interested – is very useful for helping you study.

■ Use a hyphen when you combine two words to form an adjective that goes before a noun. But *don't* use it when the adjective pair comes after the noun. For example:

> Daniel Day Lewis is a well-know actor.

but

> Daniel Day Lewis, as an actor, is well known.

■ Use a hyphen when you form a compound word from other words. For example:

> Father-in-law.

Parentheses ()

■ Use parentheses to close off a clause that would otherwise interrupt the flow of the sentence. For example:

> When you learn your punctuation rules (hopefully after you finish this section) you will be able to write well.

Learn the different parts of speech

You need to be clear about the different parts of speech. So, if you can understand how nouns, verbs or adjectives work, you will be able to judge if you are using them correctly. Here is a brief explanation of the parts of speech.

The noun

A noun is generally defined as a person, place or thing.

There are:

■ Common nouns (chair, computer, book).
■ Abstract nouns (fear, love, stress).
■ Proper nouns (John, Dublin, Westlife).
■ Collective nouns (family, crowd, flock).
■ Compound nouns (mother-in-law, aftermath).

Generally, you can test if a word is a noun by checking if you can put 'a', or 'the' before it. If you can, it's a noun.

The pronoun

A pronoun replaces a noun, when you don't want to keep repeating the noun. For example:

'John' can be replaced with 'he'.
'The dog' can be replaced with 'it'.

The adjective

An adjective is used to describe a noun. For example:

The black dog.
A fearless gangster.
This solid chair.
The game was competitive.

The verb

A verb is often referred to as an *action* or *doing* word. For example:

He walked to school.
She sings every day.

The adverb

An adverb is used to tell us more about the verb. He may have walked to school but how did he walk? The adverb will tell us. For example:

He walked briskly.
She sings sweetly.

The preposition

A preposition is used to show the relationship between two words. It generally tells us *where* something is. For example:

The cat sat on the sofa.
He stayed inside the house.
She was caught between a rock and a hard place.

The conjunction

A conjunction is used to join words, phrases or clauses. For example:

> We had fish <u>and</u> chips for dinner.
> We should know our grammar <u>but</u> it's not easy to learn all the rules.

Learn about forming sentences

Now that you know all the independent parts of speech, it's a good idea to know how they go together to form sentences.

Different parts of a sentence

Firstly let's look at the different parts of a sentence.

Every sentence must have a <u>subject</u> and <u>predicate</u>. A sentence must also always have a <u>verb</u> to be a full sentence.

The subject is who or what the sentence is about and the predicate is the rest of the sentence that is not the subject (this will include the verb). For example:

> Charles Dickens wrote many books.

Here, 'Charles Dickens' is the subject and 'wrote many books' is the predicate (including the verb 'wrote').

There are three different types of sentences:

1 Simple sentences

This type of sentence contains just one subject and predicate. For example:

> John is reading this book.

2 Complex sentences

This type of sentence is made up of a simple sentence with a dependent clause. A dependent clause is a part of the sentence that requires extra information to explain it. For example:

> Charles Dickens wrote many books, which turned out to be best sellers.

In this complex sentence, 'which turned out to be best sellers' is a dependent clause. It depends on the rest of the sentence to give it meaning.

3 Compound sentences

This type of sentence has two independent clauses usually linked by a conjunction. For example:

It was Charles Dickens's job to write but it was our job to read the books.

Here we can see that 'It was Charles Dickens's job to write' and 'it was our job to read the books' are two independent clauses put together to make up a compound sentence.

> ## Learn to avoid common mistakes in sentences

There are some very common errors people make when forming sentences. Learn to avoid these and your own sentences will improve a lot.

Subject-verb agreement

A common error in sentences is to not match your subject and your verb. This is easy to see in a simple sentence like, 'The girls was getting ready for the disco.'

Here, of course, the sentence should be: 'The girls were getting ready for the disco.'

It can be more difficult to keep track in a complex or compound sentence. For example:

Shakespeare and Dickens, both great writers who produced many volumes of work, are even more famous now than they were when they were alive.

In this sentence the 'are' and 'were' agree with the subjects, 'Shakespeare and Dickens' (they). You would *not* write: 'Shakespeare and Dickens, both great writers who produced many volumes of work, is even more famous now than they was when they was alive.'

Stay in the same verb tense

One of the most common errors in writing complex or compound sentences is to switch verb tense. For example:

'I pulled the covers over my head because I am afraid', should be: 'I pulled the cover over my head because I was afraid.'

If you start in the past tense, stay in the past tense.

Write in full sentences

You'd be surprised how many times we don't write in full sentences but remember, a sentence fragment is never a good idea, especially in a test or exam situation.

So if you are asked a question like, 'Why did Columbus explore westwards?' Don't answer: 'Because he wanted to prove the world was round.' Instead, you should write in a full sentence: 'Columbus explored westwards because he wanted to prove the world was round.'

Learn to improve your own sentences

You can give life and vibrancy to your sentences if you keep the following in mind:

Use the active not the passive voice

The active voice means writing in a more direct way. It is less formal and gives your sentences more life. For example:

> Active voice: Usher won the Entertainer of the Year Award.
> Passive voice: The Entertainer of the Year Award was won by Usher.

Choose the most appropriate, lively verb

There is a big difference between writing:

> The car came to a halt

and:

> The car screeched to a halt.

You can see that the second sentence here is more effective. It helps you picture the way the car halted and creates an atmosphere in your writing. It suggests all sorts of things like an angry driver, or a car chase. Try to always choose a verb that helps your reader picture things like this.

Show, don't tell

It is often better to show your reader emotions and feelings rather than just writing them. For example:

> It is more effective to write, 'The manager flung his baseball cap to the ground and stomped on it', than to just write, 'The manager was annoyed'.

12 Improving writing structure

By combining your knowledge of grammar, spelling, sentence structure and paragraphing, your writing will be clear, logical, interesting, lively and impressive. Here, we are going to focus on paragraphs.

The paragraph

Paragraphing serves the very important function of giving your writing order and logic. This makes it a lot easier for your reader to follow what you are trying to say.

A paragraph always contains **one main idea** or topic. The rest of the paragraph is used to illustrate further that main point with explanation or examples.

So you need to make sure that there is a main point or idea in each paragraph. The rest of the paragraph will explain that point and when you need to move on to another point, start a new paragraph.

For example:

> I was more tired than I'd ever been. My eyes ached and my body felt like it didn't belong to me. I kept taking these very deep breaths and hitting the side of my leg with the pick-handle to keep awake. I tried talking to myself but even a whisper sounded loud in the silence and I gave it up. I thought, maybe this is what it sounds like to be dead.
>
> I thought about my Mum, but it was unreal. Any other time I'd have wept for a week. I'd often imagined myself after her death…

(Taken from Brother in the Land by Robert Swindells)

The writer's first paragraph here is about his own tiredness. When he wants to change topics and write about his mother, he switches paragraphs.

Notice how you start a new paragraph by indenting, i.e. moving in a few spaces on the page.

Linking paragraphs

Paragraphs cannot stand alone in your writing. When you answer a question or write an essay, you need to write many paragraphs. Each individual paragraph should be **linked** to the next one to help your answer flow logically.

There are two ways to link paragraphs:
1   Use linking phrases.
2   Link by idea.

Linking phrases

Paragraphs can be linked to each other by beginning a following paragraph with a linking phrase. Some examples of linking phrases would be:

Table 12.1: Linking phrases	
For example,	On the other hand,
Similarly,	In contrast,
But,	However,
In the same way,	Conversely,

For example:

> Within a minute they were gone. As soon as the motorcade was out of sight, I turned to my parents and said, 'That was nothing.'
>
>   But, of course, in retrospect, that fleeting glimpse of John and Jacqueline Kennedy was truly something…

Notice that these two paragraphs are linked when the second one begins with 'But, of course'. It helps the writing flow from one paragraph to the next and makes the chain of thoughts seem natural.

Linking by idea

A second way to link paragraphs is to have them flow with the natural train of thought or by ideas.

For example:

Look again at our paragraphs from *Brother in the Land*.

> I was more tired than I'd ever been. My eyes ached and my body felt like it didn't belong to me. I kept taking these very deep breaths and hitting the side of my leg with the pick-handle to keep awake. I tried talking to myself but even a whisper sounded loud in the silence and I gave it up. I thought, maybe this is what it sounds like to be dead.
>
>   I thought about my Mum, but it was unreal. Any other time I'd have wept for a week. I'd often imagined myself after her death.....

(Taken from Brother in the Land by Robert Swindells)

Notice how the second paragraph naturally flows from the first one because it is an expected chain of thought that when he mentioned death in the first paragraph, he immediately thought of his dead mother. This is linking the paragraphs by the natural flow of ideas.

A good opening paragraph

A good opening paragraph to an exam answer can be very effective. It will set the right tone for a clear answer and impress an examiner.

The best opening paragraph will introduce what your answer is going to be about. If necessary, it will also state your stance on the question (i.e. say whether you agree with a statement or belief or not).

For example, imagine you are asked the following question on a novel you have read as part of your English course:

> From a novel you have read discuss a character that you admired.

Your opening paragraph for an answer to this should look something like this:

> *The novel I have chosen is **To Kill a Mockingbird** by Harper Lee. In this novel I admired the character Atticus, Jem and Scout's father. He displayed many admirable qualities throughout the novel like solid Christian values, fatherly love, fairness and bravery.*

You can see that this opening begins by naming the novel and character the student aims to write about. It also sums up the main points the student will make in his answer about Atticus.

A good concluding paragraph

A good concluding paragraph will sum up your main points again and round off your answer.

For example, a concluding paragraph for your *To Kill a Mockingbird* answer might be:

> *As we have seen, Atticus possessed a lot of admirable qualities that made me like him. He was fair and kind to all his neighbours; he defended a black man at a time when this was frowned upon in America; he showed his bravery in killing the rabid dog and in standing up to the mob; and throughout the novel he showed his love for his children. It was easy to admire this character.*

This paragraph sums up the main points the student would have made in his answer.

Improving your own paragraphs

Keep them clear and easy to read

The best paragraphs will be clear and easy to read. You don't need to try and use big, impressive words. Keep your language simple and write in a clear and logical manner, so that your paragraph will be effective.

Mix short sentences with long ones

Generally, the best paragraphs will have a mixture of longer and shorter sentences. Take a look back at the concluding paragraph we read for the *To Kill a Mockingbird* answer. This paragraph has one very long sentence listing Atticus's qualities but it's followed by a very short sentence. This mixes up the sentence structures and makes it easier and more interesting for the reader.

13 Building your vocabulary

Your ability to express yourself both verbally and in writing is directly related to the extent of your vocabulary. If you have a broad range of words at your disposal, you can easily express your thoughts in interesting and diverse ways.

In its simplest terms, you need a range of words to use in your writing in order to avoid that awful habit of repetition. Often a student will write an otherwise good answer, which will be ruined by the student's repetition of the same word throughout the answer. A student might want to say that a character in a play was angry … and later in the play he was also angry … and in the last act of the play he was angry …

This repetition of 'angry' could be avoided with a broader vocabulary. How about using alternative words like *furious, enraged, incensed, ireful, indignant,* or *wrathful*?

You can see that if you have a stable of words to draw from, you can make your writing more varied and therefore more interesting.

So how can you build up a store of words?

Read, read, read

Extensive reading is the best way to learn new words. Read lots of different material: books, magazines, newspapers, advertisements, brochures, etc. When you read, take note of any new words you like the sound of and write them down. Review these words regularly and try to use them in an essay of your own.

It can be a good idea to write the word on a cue or flash card with the definition at the back. Include a sample sentence here also. If you do this, you learn how to spell the word, its meaning and its use all at once. Continue to use the flash card until you feel totally comfortable with using the word.

Use a dictionary

A dictionary should be your constant companion when you read. Whenever you come across a word you don't understand, look the meaning up in the dictionary, take note of the word and definition. Learn that word and try to use it in your own writing.

Use a thesaurus

A thesaurus is a another useful reference book you should keep on hand. If you find yourself repeating one particular word over and over in your writing, then look it up in the thesaurus and find an alternative word you could use instead.

Transfer words from one subject to another

Quite often, you will learn new words in a subject like Science, Business Studies or Geography. Try to use the new word in another subject or in another context. For example, early in your Business Studies class you learn the word 'entrepreneur' (someone who sets up a new business). This might be a new word for you. So you learn it and later, in English class, you are asked to write an essay about a person you admire, so you write about your father, the entrepreneur!

Learn one new word per day

Aim to learn at least one new word per day. Learn its spelling and meaning and then try to use it as soon as you can in your writing. The sooner you start to use it in your everyday writing, the better. You can help your memory by writing it on a flash card and reviewing it every day until you feel you know it well.

Practise, practise, practise

Next time you see a very young child who is just learning to talk, notice how he or she learns new words. The child will repeat a new word many times and continue to use it until he or she feels comfortable with this new word.

This is what you need to do. When you learn a new word, continue to review it and use it as often as you can until you feel comfortable with it. In this way, you will not forget any new words and they will become an everyday part of your vocabulary.

Some quick dos and don'ts of building up your vocabulary

Do	Don't
Stay alert to new words.	Rely on the same word all the time.
Do decide to learn a new word per day.	Be satisfied with what you already know.
Use flash cards as a learning aid.	Dismiss the dictionary and thesaurus.
Use the new word as soon and as often as you can.	

Some quick dos and don'ts of writing skills

Do	Don't
Take an active interest in your own writing; learn to correct your own mistakes.	Rely on teachers to correct everything.
Keep a list of words to learn.	Continue to make the same mistakes.
Learn the rules of spelling.	Dismiss grammar and punctuation as unimportant.
Learn grammar and punctuation rules.	Develop an allergy to dictionaries.
Structure correctly.	Think that spelling errors don't matter.
Keep writing simple and clear.	
Try to build up your vocabulary.	

Section 5

How to Do Well in Exams

Of course, all the work you are doing is leading to a key aim: succeeding in your exams. This section guides you through the process of preparing for your exams, doing the actual exams, and what to do once the exams are over.

What you will learn in Section 5

In this section you will learn:
- general study tips and techniques for practising exam questions
- how to manage the exam itself
- how to identify the types of questions and vocabulary used in exams
- how to get organised before the exam
- how to stay calm and focused during the exam
- what not to do after the exam
- how to prepare for oral exams
- how to prepare for aural exams.

14 Preparing for exams

Practice makes perfect

When you are studying, it makes sense that the only real way to prepare for those exams is to practise them. A huge amount of your learning, especially coming nearer the exams, revolves around trying exam questions. This is where you put your learning into practice. For some subjects like Maths and sections of Business Studies, actually doing the calculations is the only way to learn effectively. For this you'll need to refine your practising skills.

Answer blind

Answering blind is when you revise a section from your textbook and notes and then put everything away. Find a question relating to this section from past exam papers and try to answer it without looking at any notes. Answer in full exam format and when you feel you've done all you can correct it with the help of your book and notes.

You can also do this in relation to homework. Think of homework as a test, especially in something like Maths. Try to complete the homework without your books and then consult them once you've answered the question to check your answer or make adjustments.

Time answers

It's very important that you can answer a question in the time you will have available in the exam for that type of question. When you answer blind, make sure you time yourself and then check against the recommended time. If you are very much under the time allowed, you'll probably need to do some more study on this section in order to be able to build up your answer a little more. If you are over the time, you need to work on planning your answer more effectively.

Use marking schemes

When an examiner corrects an exam paper, they have a marking scheme to help them. This marking scheme tells them what to expect in the answer. You can make use of these marking schemes to help in your answering of past papers. You can find marking schemes on http://www.examinations.ie, where you will get them under 'Examination Material Archive'.

After you've attempted a question blind, use the marking scheme for that question to help you correct your answer. You will learn a lot about where you could have improved your answer and it will give you an insight into what the examiners look for.

Rework mock papers

When you get your mock paper back, make full use of it. Rework the questions you already answered, based on your teacher's comment or the marking scheme, which the teacher will be able to give you. You should also work through some of the other questions you rejected in the actual test for added practice on other options you may have to take in June. For example, in English you will only have answered on one poet in the mock exam, so now choose one of the other poets and use the marking scheme to help your practice and learning.

Follow examples

When you're practising mathematical-type problems, go back to your class notes and find a problem you know is correct. Rework this question without looking back at your original answer. When you're finished, correct against the original. Now find a similar one in the exam papers and work through that one. Continue to work through similar problems until you feel confident you have mastered this section.

Piece together solutions

When you're trying to learn the steps involved in solving a mathematical-type problem, work one through correctly, and cut up the answer to leave one step per piece of paper. Now leave it aside for a while, then come back to it and piece together the steps in the correct order.

Work with friends

Work on mathematical problems with a friend or group of friends. One person should start the solution and complete Step 1, pass to the next person who completes Step 2, pass along again and complete Step 3. Continue passing the solution around (or back and forth if there are just two of you) until it is completed. Start another problem; this time a different person begins.

For some advice on working as part of a group, see Chapter 4, 'Motivating yourself'.

Make use of revision books

Revision books can be good guides to the important topics in a subject. Work through any questions in the book and check the answers against those provided in the book or against your textbook.

Work with your teachers

When you practise a question from an exam paper or book, feel free to ask your teacher to look over it for you. Ask for any comments on where you might improve and make sure you put those into practice next time round. Don't be afraid to approach teachers; they always admire initiative.

15 Doing exams

So you've done your study and you want to display your knowledge to the examiner. The best way to do that is to see the exam as a type of game where a good strategy will get you the results you want. That strategy will ensure that you answer the questions you are actually asked and that you give the examiners the information they are looking for in a clear and logical way.

If you want to approach the exam logically and methodically, you will need to manage your time and method in a strict way.

Reading the paper

Read the entire paper

Before even thinking about putting pen to paper, read the entire exam paper. Read all the questions carefully and, in the case of comprehending sections, all the reading material.

Read instructions

Even if you know what you need to answer on the paper, always read all the instructions carefully. Make sure you're clear about what's expected – such as the number of questions you need to answer and which sections have choices. This will help ease the nerves a little and help focus your mind on the task ahead.

Choosing your questions

Mark off questions

Mark off the questions you definitely what to answer. These will be the ones you know you feel comfortable with. When you've answered these and you still need to choose a few more, read back over the choices you have left and take the ones you know the most about. To decide this, it might be a good idea to jot down a few ideas for your answers and then choose the ones you have more ideas for.

Check marks allocated

Always check the amount of marks allocated to each question. This will give you a guide as to how long your answer needs to be. As a rough rule of thumb, you can generally think of 10 marks as meaning a paragraph. So, a 30-mark answer will require a long answer of at least 3 full paragraphs. On the other hand a 2-mark question will only require a line or two. Never spend too long on a lower mark question; you need to save your time for the ones with more marks at stake.

Understand the task given

Read the question very carefully and be clear about what you are being asked. If you're asked to *outline* something, then think about what outline means and follow that instruction. (You can find out more about different question vocabulary in Chapter 16 below.) Re-read the question and highlight the important words in it, just to keep clear in your mind what you need to focus on.

Writing answers

Plan your answer

Always, always plan what you will write about, especially in essay-type answers. You can do this by 'brainstorming' ideas. This means jotting down the ideas that come into your mind with regard to the question asked. Jot down short words and phrases to keep these ideas in your mind. Take those rough notes then and decide the order of paragraphing you will use.

Stick to the question asked

One of the major mistakes made by students in exams is not answering the question asked. You must stick to the task you are given, which does not mean trying to fit in an answer you have already learned off or putting down on paper everything you know about a topic. Make sure you understand what the question is looking for and then stick to that. Plan your answer around the question asked and stay focused on this.

Time your answers

Before the exam you should have figured out how long you can afford to spend on each answer/section. Stick to these time limits. If you are not finished an answer but your time is up, leave space in your answer book and move on to the next answer. You will probably have time at the end of the exam to come back and finish this answer. But always move on at the end of your time limit because if you spend too long on this one answer and then don't get time to start your last one, you will lose all the marks of the last one; however, if you even get half of one done and two-thirds of the last one, you can get some marks for both answers.

Don't waste time

Don't waste valuable time with things you won't get marks for like writing out the questions or highlighting quotes. Save your time for the important task: writing answers.

Number answers

Always number your answers clearly, making sure your number corresponds with the one on the paper. Put the number clearly in the margin of the answer book and then put your answer to the right of the margin. Do not answer a question within this margin; leave it only for answer numbers.

Answer all the questions!

Make sure you answer all the questions you should answer. Never, never leave a blank space where an answer should be. You can't get marks for nothing but you might get some marks for an attempt. So always make an attempt at every question.

Be careful also to answer all the different parts in a question. If there are three or four different sections to the question, make sure you answer all three or four. Double check that you did this before you move on to the next question. Be aware also that there might be choices within these sections, so stay alert to that.

Keep answer book neat

Try to keep your answer book neat and easy to read. Write in the best handwriting you can manage and skip lines between answers. Write titles or headings on your work and underline them. Write lists with numbers and each item on a new line. Paragraph clearly, indenting your new paragraph away from the margin.

Keep busy

If you're having difficulty with a question and feel yourself getting bogged down, then leave space to come back to the question later and move on for now – you can always come back to it later. But for now keep busy and go on to answer the next question you like. The process of keeping busy writing is great for confidence.

Writing exam answers

Keep lists organised

If you're asked to write a list of items or instructions, make sure this list is clear and logical. Write a title on the top and use numbered or bulleted points, changing to a new line with each new point.

Keep essays organised

Begin essay-type answers with a short and clear introduction that tells the reader what your answer will be about. This should state your stance (i.e. whether you agree with the statement in the question or not) and say briefly what the main points of your essay will be.

The rest of your essay should then be divided into clear, logical paragraphs. Move to a new paragraph when you move to a new point or idea. (You can find out more about paragraphing in Chapter 12 above.)

Finish off your essay with a short conclusion, once again summing up the main points you have made.

Avoid summaries

It is very easy to drift away from the question and lapse into a summary. For example, in English you might be asked to discuss how a certain poet appeals to a younger reader. Here you need to discuss how that poet's poems can be of interest to young people. However, many students will lapse into summarising what each poem is *about*, which is not what you've been asked to do. Be careful to focus on answering the question, not summarise.

Back up your points

When you make a particular point, always back that point up. This means that you support your answer by using:

1   examples
2   quotes
3   references to a reading passage or other material.

If you want to use an **example**, imagine you are answering a Business Studies question on insurance. You are discussing contribution. You are explaining that when a person takes out insurance with more than one company, each company will pay compensation in proportion to the amount of the total risk that they covered.

Now the best way to explain this point and back it up is to give an example. You give the example that you insure a house with two different companies: with one company for €160,000 and with the second company for €20,000. Now when you suffer damage worth €20,000, Company 1 will pay €16,000 and Company 2 will pay €4,000. The use of the example shows the examiner that you know exactly what you are talking about and helps you explain the concept fully.

Another way to back up your points is to use **quotes**. Say you are in your English exam and you want to discuss the novel *Of Mice and Men*. In your answer, you want to make the point that the ranch workers in the story have a lonely life. To back up this point you could use the quote from George where he says, 'Guys like us, that work on ranches, are the loneliest guys in the world. They got no family. They don't belong no place.' The use of the quote lends force to your point and impresses the examiner that you know exactly what you are talking about and that you can focus your answers on the novel in question.

A third way to back up your ideas is to **reference the material** you have learned. For example, imagine you are in your History exam. You have been asked to discuss the idea that the state of the German economy after World War I contributed to the rise of Hitler. Here you may want to reference the Treaty of Versailles of 1919 where Germany was punished for its role in World War I. Your reference to the treaty helps back up your ideas that the German people became bitter and impoverished after World War I and this aided Hitler's rise to power.

Some quick dos and don'ts of written exam techniques

Do	Don't
Answer the question asked.	Begin answering without a plan.
Stick to the point.	Write down everything you know.
Pay attention to question vocabulary.	Summarise (unless asked).
Back up points.	

Towards the end of the exam

Read through the paper again

Before you take the last read through your paper, go back to any questions you might have skipped over. Try some kind of answer. Never leave a blank space.

Read over answers and proofread your paper

Always allow time to read back over your answers. This will help you spot inconsistencies and grammar errors that you can correct. In addition, other ideas may come to you as you read back over your answers, which you can fill in now.

Reading over something you have written and checking for errors is called 'proofreading'; it's a good idea to practise this skill for exams. The secret to good proofreading is to learn to read *every single word* carefully. This may sound like obvious advice but in our normal reading we tend to skip over every third or fourth word, especially the small ones. Practise reading each word out loud at first until you get used to this new way of reading. Soon you may surprise yourself and proofread at your normal reading speed.

So, in order to proofread your paper:

- Check that your spellings are correct to the best of your knowledge.
- Check that the sentences make sense and that you have followed rules like subject-verb agreement.
- Make sure your spelling and use of words are consistent throughout your exam paper. Words that can be written legitimately in two different ways should not swap and change as your answer continues. For example, decide whether you will use 'realise' or 'realize' and keep them consistent.

■ Imagine you are the examiner and think about whether your answer makes sense overall or not. Have you argued your point well? Could you add in any more relevant information? Have you answered the actual question asked?

Check against instructions

Finally check once again, against the instructions, that you have completed everything you should have completed. Count how many questions you have answered and make sure that you have answered all sections within each question.

Include all material

When you are sealing your answer book for collection, make sure you include all pages on which you answered questions, like the actual exam paper and extra answer books. Check too that you have filled in the front of the answer book and especially check that your exam number is correct.

Some quick dos and don'ts of managing the exam	
Do	**Don't**
Read the entire paper first.	Forget to read back over your answers at the end.
Choose questions carefully.	Forget to include the exam paper if you've answered questions on it.
Pay attention to marks.	
Stay within time constraints.	
Answer all parts of all questions.	

16 Understanding exam language

It's essential in exams that you read questions very carefully and are clear that you understand exactly what you're being asked to do. Some questions will ask for just facts while others will ask for your own opinion and you need to be sure which is which.

In addition, you need to recognise the different kinds of tasks set with regard to the vocabulary of the question. For example, there will be no need to write an essay-type answer if you are asked to *list* a set of reasons; here you are being asked to make out a numbered list, not write a discursive essay.

Learn the different types of possible questions and the question vocabulary and you won't go wrong. You will also save time and give the examiner what he or she is looking for.

Types of questions

Information-retrieval questions

These questions require that you retrieve information. They are looking for factual answers. They will usually start with 'What?' For example, 'What were the main developments in art during the Renaissance?' is an information retrieval question because you are being asked to give *facts* about the main developments in art in the Renaissance. You are not required to give an opinion, just list the developments. For these questions, you simply need to access or find the information and write it out in your own words in a clear, logical way.

Opinion questions

These are questions where you will be required to give your own opinion. For example, 'Do you think King Lear is a man more sinned against than sinning?' is an opinion question because you have to give your own opinion on what you think of King Lear. Always make sure that you back up that opinion with reference back to facts you have learned, in this case from the play, *King Lear*.

Not all opinion questions will begin as clearly with 'In your opinion' or 'Do you think?' They may be stated something like this: 'To what extent did The Second Vatican Council change the Catholic Church in an important way?' This is an opinion question also because here you will have to give an opinion on whether you think it had a big effect or not.

Style questions

These will appear on the language papers and are based on the style of the writer. Here you are required to analyse, and often give an opinion on, the way the writer writes. Examples of style questions would be 'How does the writer persuade you?' or 'Does the writer succeed in cresting a tense atmosphere in the first paragraph?' In order to answer these types of questions you need to discuss the way the writer puts the passage together; things like the beginning and ending and how the paragraphs are constructed; his or her use of certain words; description elements; creation of setting; and so on.

Question vocabulary

Pay close attention to the vocabulary used in the question. When you are asked to *outline* something, this is very different to when you are asked to *evaluate*. So be aware of these differences and stick to what you're asked to do.

Here is a list of the most common question vocabulary you'll come across.

Analyse

Take each element of the question or statement or passage and consider all explanations. Examine in detail how something is put together.

Comment

Write an explanatory note, explaining the concept questioned and giving an opinion on it.

Compare

Take each of the things you have been asked to compare and show the similarities between them.

Contrast

Take each of the things you have been asked to contrast and show the differences between them.

Define

Give the exact meaning, in your own words, of a statement or word.

Describe

Explain the concept questioned in your own words. Give details of the characteristics of the item questioned.

Discuss

Explain all aspects of what you have been asked to discuss in your own words and give details with examples.

Distinguish

Take each of the elements you are asked to distinguish and show the differences between them.

Draft

This means that you should draw up what you have been asked to draft.

Evaluate

Discuss fully what you have been asked to evaluate and then give an opinion.

Explain

Give a detailed account in your own words of the idea questioned. Clarify all aspects of the statement.

Identify

List and outline briefly the points asked for.

Illustrate

Explain a point in your own words and back your answer up with an example.

List

Give a numbered list of items or words without any detailed explanation.

Select

Simply name the items you are asked to select.

State

Just clearly and briefly give the main points without any detailed explanations.

Trace

Explain the argument/description, in your own words, in a logical order from beginning to end.

Outline

Give only the main points in your own words without any detailed analysis.

17 How to stay calm before, during and after exams

It can be difficult to stay focused and relatively relaxed immediately before and during an exam. Even after the exam you may feel stressed and worried about your performance. But if you read the suggestions I make below, you can get through the exams with ease.

The day before the exam

In that day before the exam many students panic. They worry about what they have not done, about forgetting what they have done and stress levels can often build up so much that it freezes the mind. Follow some basic steps to staying focused and stress free in the day before the exam.

Post up your timetable

Make sure you have your exam timetable posted up in a prominent position in the house, maybe in the kitchen on the fridge or on a notice board by the door. You will now have it for easy reference of dates and times.

Check date and time

Always check and double check the date and time of your exam. You'd be surprised how many people do strange things around exam time, like turn up on the wrong day or time.

Stop studying

The day before the exam is not the time to learn new things. You can take the day to go over notes, especially cue cards, but otherwise you should not attempt to learn anything new at this stage. If you have organised your time efficiently up to now, you will have covered everything in time, so this day should just be for recapping on main points you want to remember like quotes, or lists of ideas.

Concentrate today on what you *do* know; you can't change now what you don't know.

Get organised

Gather together all the supplies you'll need for the next day's exam(s). Here's a list of the general ones you'll need for all or most exams:

Table 17.1: Exam equipment		
– Pens: lots of blue/black ones and some other coloured ones like red and green.	– Tippex. – Pencil eraser. – Pencil sharpener.	
– Pencils: for drawing diagrams.	– Paper clips. – Ruler.	
– Coloured pencils: for diagrams. – Water and chewy sweets.	– Calculator. – Other Maths supplies like compass, protractor, set square etc.	

(Remember though to double check that there are not any more special equipment items you might need for a specific exam, like log tables for Maths etc.)

Put your supplies into a bag or pencil case and leave them ready to go the next day. This way you won't have to worry about forgetting something in the morning.

Make sure also that your clothes are out and ready for the morning – whether it is a choice of clothes or your school uniform.

Of course, when we're in bed many of us start thinking of things we may have forgotten and remember something we need when we're lying awake at 1 a.m. The worry then of forgetting in the morning can keep us awake. The best way to deal with this is to have a pen and notepad beside the bed and just jot down anything your want to remember. Now you can relax and know that you won't forget in the morning because you'll have your note.

Have lots of water available to bring with you, as you will want to stay hydrated in the exam and being thirsty is very distracting. You may also want to have a roll of chewy sweets as the chewing can help concentration.

Now that you have everything ready to go you won't be rushing around in the morning gathering stuff.

Take the evening off

Finish up any last-minute review of notes early in the evening and do something relaxing like taking a long walk or having a relaxing bath.

Listen to music

Music can be very relaxing, so make sure you listen to some of the easy-listening variety this evening. Try to lose yourself in the music and clear your mind of quotes or facts or dates.

Talk it out

If you're feeling panicky, talk it over with a parent or friend. They can offer, at the very least, an ear and, at the most, reassurance that you have studied well and that you are prepared.

Reassure yourself

Reassure yourself that you have studied well by thinking about all the hours you have dedicated to this subject. Remind yourself of how well you have done in past tests or how much work you have put in since your last test to improve on that score. Tell yourself that you know this subject and that you are well prepared.

Use motivating statements like, 'I know this subject', 'I can do well', 'I am well prepared.'

Exercise

If you're feeling particularly tense do some relaxing exercises before bed. Try the ones you'll find in Chapter 1, 'Keeping well' for relieving tension and stress.

Take an early night

Go to bed early and get a good night's sleep. You need to go into the exam refreshed and rested. Pulling an all-nighter study session is never a good idea.

Sleeping isn't always easy though when you have an exam on your mind. Your mind can start racing and you mightn't be able to stop thinking about what you have learned or not learned. Get rid of those panicky feelings by clearing your mind and relaxing your body. Try this exercise for doing that:

1   Lie flat on your back and close your eyes.
2   Give all your concentration and focus to your toes.
3   Now imagine there are weights hanging from each toe pulling them down into the bed.
4   When you feel your toes relaxing, concentrate on your ankles.
5   Imagine weights hanging from these pulling them down into the mattress.
6   When you feel the muscles relax move up to your calves.
7   Continue to repeat this process all the way up your body; although it's highly unlikely you'll get to your head, you'll be asleep by then.

The day of the exam

Get up early

On the morning of the exam, get up early and leave yourself lots of time to get ready. Rushing on the morning of an exam will only add to your stress levels, so make sure you allow plenty of time for breakfast and the journey.

Eat a healthy breakfast

Eat a good healthy breakfast before you leave. It may be difficult, but try to eat something. If you eat slowly and deliberately, it will be a little easier. This is vital because if you're hungry in the exam it will hinder your concentration and recall.

Eggs are a good option, as they have good energy content and are reputed to be good 'brain food'. Eat them with wholemeal bread. Alternatively, some cereal and toast with marmalade is a good option. Don't drink too much tea or coffee because caffeine dehydrates the body and this is not good for concentration. Go for fresh fruit juice instead.

Arrive early

Arrive a little early for your exam: about 15 minutes before you are due to begin is best. Again, rushing in at the last minute can be stressful and it can take some time to settle down and get the brain functioning. Find your seat and put your supplies on your desk. Take a few minutes then to have a stroll around or listen to music on your MP3 player to help relax you.

Don't talk about study

Don't let yourself get dragged into conversations with your friends about what you did and didn't study. It's often best just to sit quietly and listen to music than to compare notes at this stage. What if someone says, 'I think Eavan Boland's coming up on the paper' and you haven't studied Eavan Boland? You'll panic. So it's best to avoid these kinds of conversations. What you have studied you have studied and you can't change it now anyway, so there's no need to panic yourself.

In the case of oral exams, don't ask the candidates before you what the examiner asked them. Chances are your conversation with the examiner will be very different and it can only dishearten you to hear that they have been asked something you have not prepared well. It's a no-win situation, so avoid it.

Don't change levels

You should have decided on what level (higher or ordinary) you're taking in each exam long before today. Usually, this is best done immediately after the mock exams. Work with your teacher to make this decision. Take the teacher's advice seriously but ultimately it has to be your decision.

However, often students will panic at the last minute and take a lower paper. Try to avoid this. If you've put in the work, you should do the level you've prepared for. If you change at this stage you'll probably spend the entire exam worrying about whether you made the right decision or not, so it's better to stick with your original decision and go for it.

During the exam

The aim here is to stay focused and relaxed. Concentrate on one step at a time and on putting all that you have learned into practice.

Have water and sweets with you

Make sure you bring a bottle of water with you, as you'll want to stay hydrated. The weather can often be very warm those first few weeks in June, so the importance of water can't be overemphasised. It's best to avoid fizzy drinks, as they will actually add to dehydration.

You might also want to have a roll of chewy sweets with you, as the process of chewing can often be good for concentration.

Ask for spare paper

Ask your supervisor for a spare piece of paper you can use for rough notes. When you come across a question where you need to recall information you learned using one of the memory tricks from Chapter 9, use this paper to write out the information. For example, if you need to recall sources of finance for Business Studies and you used the acronym CREST TOP, then write this out and fill in the words. Use these words then as a basis for your answer.

Relax your breathing

Before you open the exam paper, close your eyes and take slow, regular breaths. Even if your heart is racing, keep up the slow, regular breaths and your heart rate will slow down. When you feel in control, open your eyes and start reading the paper.

Manage the exam

Follow the exam techniques you learned in Chapter 15, 'Doing exams'. Reading the entire paper first can help ease you into the exam. Choose your easiest questions first and build up your confidence by doing the ones you feel certain about. Answer all questions, stick to the question asked and read back over you paper at the end.

Stay positive

Remain positive. Even if you come across a question you're not sure about, skip over it for now and continue on. Keep reminding yourself of how much you know and how well you are doing on the questions you know well. When you have to answer the question you are less certain about, begin with what you do know. Brainstorm all you know about that topic/section and then put your answer together based on that.

Unblock your mind

Have you ever panicked in an exam when you couldn't immediately think of the answer to a question? If you have, you probably found that this blocked your mind even more, and you began to feel that you couldn't think at all. If this does happen to you in an exam, you can use a simple 'free writing' exercise to help unblock your mind:

1   Read the question carefully.
2   Take your rough work piece of paper and start writing down anything you know about that topic questioned.
3   Just write anything relating to that topic, even if it has nothing to do with the question.
4   This allows you to free up your mind and this usually leads to other thoughts on the topic.
5   Eventually, when your mind is flowing more freely you can begin to access information you need for this specific question.

If you feel particularly tense and can't think straight at all, then just start to write anything at all. Just start to write. Don't worry about what you write – just write. A few minutes of this should help you calm down and soon you will notice coherent thought returning. Now focus back on the question and see where it takes you.

Reign back in concentration

Exams can be very long and it is understandable that your concentration will slip occasionally. So you need to be able to reign it back in. The best way to do this is to engage in *active reading*. When you read passages on the paper stay active by highlighting important words and phrases; finding answers to questions and constantly asking yourself, what was the main point of that paragraph.

When you need to concentrate on reading a question, take a highlighter and highlight the important words in the question. Ask yourself: what exactly is the question looking for?

If you find yourself feeling particularly distracted, sit back for moment, close your eyes and concentrate totally on your breathing. Breath in slow, regular breaths until your feel more relaxed. Open your eyes and look again at the paper with fresh eyes.

Don't give up

Never give up on a question you should answer and leave it blank. You can't get any marks for blank paper but you might get some marks for an attempt. So always try every question. Even when you are unsure of the answer write what you know about the topic.

Take all the time available

Don't leave early. Take all the time available to you and read through your answers before handing up your paper. Often, other information will come to you as you read back over your answer and you can fill this in. You have one shot at sitting this paper, so you might as well make the most of it.

Take bathroom breaks

You are allowed to go to the bathroom during the exam, so if you feel the need to go, go. Leaving it off will only affect your concentration negatively. You just need to make sure you raise your arm, ask for permission and the attendant will have to go with you.

After the exam

You'd be forgiven for thinking that once you leave the exam all your worries are over and you can wave bye bye to stress. But this is not always the case. Students often feel down and stressed after an exam, uttering the words 'should have' and torturing themselves about what they did and didn't write. Don't let yourself fall into this trap. Stay positive and move on are the buzz phrases here.

Avoid post-mortems

It's tempting to go over the entire paper with your friends comparing your answers to each section but this is never a good idea. Hearing what other people wrote can be very dejecting. You can begin to doubt your own interpretation of the questions and what if you find out for certain that you were wrong? Can you do anything about it? No, you will only torture yourself and undermine your confidence. So avoid post-mortems!

Talking about the paper is a good idea though, but you should do this with someone who hasn't just sat the exam. Talk to a parent or a friend who wasn't there. Talk your way through the paper and then drop the subject. You can't change anything now, so once you've cleared your mind of any concerns you may have, it's time to put it behind you.

Focus on the positive

Remind yourself of the positive aspects of the exam. Think about the questions you feel you did well on. Congratulate yourself for sitting the exam successfully.

Move on

Lingering on thoughts of an exam you can no longer do anything about is not healthy. Try to put it behind you now and move on to your next challenge.

Set up a routine for yourself for moving on. For example, your routine might be to go home, gather all your books and notes relating to that exam and put them away in a press. Then tick off that exam off your exam timetable. Now you know you're finished with that one.

Reward yourself

Reward yourself for getting through the exam by treating yourself to something you enjoy – maybe your favourite lunch or meeting up with a friend.

De-stress

Clear your mind and de-stress after the exam by doing some exercise like walking or cycling. Do some relaxation exercises if you're still feeling stressed. The ones for relieving tension and stress in Chapter 1, 'Keeping well', are good options.

Some quick dos and don'ts of before, during and after the exam	
Do	**Don't**
Stay positive.	Attempt to learn anything new at this late stage.
Double check dates and times.	Go into the exam without proper equipment.
Organise supplies.	Pull an all-nighter.
Relax.	Let yourself get dehydrated.
Use memory tricks learned.	Do a post-mortem.
Use free writing techniques.	Give up.
Answer all questions.	
Move on.	

18 Preparing for oral exams

This section presumes that the oral exams you're preparing for are language ones. In these language exams you will be expected to speak in a different language and understand the examiner as he or she speaks to you in this language.

The secret to learning a language is to *immerse yourself* in it. This means speaking it and listening to it as often as you can. So, when you want to prepare for an oral exam you need to use a language as much as possible.

Preparation strategies

Prepare early

Begin preparation for your oral exam as early as possible. This will give you time to get comfortable with the language. If you leave it too late, you might get panicky and then it becomes more difficult to cram everything in.

This preparation will, of course, also be of great help in preparing for the aural and written exams, so this work serves three purposes and is worth doing well.

Commit to language time

Make a commitment that you will speak the language you're learning for at least 15 minutes every day. Meet up with or call a friend who is also learning this language and exchange all your news in, for example, French. The more you use the language, the more comfortable you'll become with it and the more it will flow like a natural conversation, which is what you're aiming for.

Speak to the mirror

Master pronunciation by speaking to the mirror. Pay attention to how the words are formed with your lips and tongue until you feel comfortable with new pronunciations. This also gets you used to hearing your voice out loud as you master a language.

Speak your teacher's language

Try to always speak to your language teacher in the language you're learning. Greet them and answer everything you can in class in that language. Even when you meet them in the hallway, why not speak, for example, German?

Check pronunciation

Check pronunciations with your teacher. Never go ahead and learn a word or phrase without checking that you have the correct pronunciation and use. It can be very difficult to go back and re-learn something you think you already know how to pronounce, so it's better to put the effort into getting it right first time round.

Listen very carefully to how your teacher pronounces new words and even double check common terms like 'et' in French – you'd be surprised how you can fall into the wrong pronunciation and not be able to adjust it.

This will entail good listening skills, which you can review in Chapter 7, 'Learning to listen'.

Reinforce lessons

Reinforce what you have learned in class that day by using it that evening. If, for example, you discovered how to talk about your favourite music group, then tonight you need to practise that (either with your mirror or with a friend) and learn the related vocabulary. Do this as soon after the lesson as possible and then recap the next day and the next weeks. Don't let all this build up until just before the exam; the faster you use it, the easier it will be to remember it.

Learn vocabulary

Group vocabulary in topics-related categories. For example, if you want to learn to speak about your family, then list vocabulary you will need like father, mother, brother, sister and so on. You can then use the memory tricks you learned in Chapter 9 and the vocabulary – building tips you read of in Chapter 13 to learn and retain these words and phrases. Use this vocabulary as much as you can in your language time each day.

You will find the vocabulary-building tips in Chapter 13 helpful in building up a foreign vocabulary, so check these out again.

Prepare topics, not just vocabulary

Students will often learn off lots of vocabulary for something like hobbies. They will know lots of different hobbies and could list them if needed. However, you need to keep in mind that you should also be able to discuss the hobbies in some detail. Be prepared to discuss the topic fully. Don't resort to just listing things in the exam: talk about the topic.

Checking pronunciation

Tape yourself

It's a good idea to tape/record yourself speaking the language you're learning. This has three main advantages:

1   It will help ease your anxiety about having a tape recorder in front of you while you speak, which you will have in the exam.
2   You will be able to check how your pronunciation sounds while you speak and you can remedy any mispronunciations. If you're unsure about how something sounds, ask your teacher to check it for you and direct you in the right way.
3   You will see where your problem areas are and where you are missing enough vocabulary or thoughts on a particular topic. You can then work on these weaker areas.

At some stage during the year, your language teacher will have an individual practice with you in conversational language. Ask them to tape this for you and listen back carefully to their corrections of your pronunciations, verb tenses, etc. Learn from the experience. The same applies to your mock oral exam.

Videotape yourself

If you can, it's a good idea to videotape yourself speaking the language you're learning. You will get used to seeing yourself speak it and you'll be able to hear the way you are pronouncing words better this way. It helps to get you less afraid of the language and of speaking it out loud.

Listen to the language

Listen to as much of the language as you can:
■   Watch films in your chosen language.
■   Watch TV programmes in this language.

- Get some language CDs and listen to them frequently. Repeat the phrases as you hear them.
- If possible, exchange language time with a native speaker – you'll speak English with them one day, if they speak German with you the next day.

Write out answers

Prepare topics by writing out answers to possible questions. This will help you form thoughts on the topic and you can ask your teacher to look over it before you go ahead and learn it.

Practise your set pieces

In most oral exams, there will be a section where you read or speak about something you have prepared before the exam, like a reading passage, photo or project.

- Practise these pieces very frequently. Go through them first with your teacher, who will make sure you are going in the right direction and that you are pronouncing everything correctly.
- Prepare any vocabulary you will need for answering questions.
- Prepare a likely list of questions and practise answering them.
- Try then to set up the exam conditions with someone in front of you and a tape recorder. Now practise your set piece this way.

Practise online

There are many very good websites out there that you can use for practising languages. You can find sites with interactive lessons and quizzes and puzzles. Ask your teacher to recommend sites in your particular language, or just do an online search for relevant sites.

The exam day

Avoid discussions

On the day of the exam, when your friends come out of their orals, avoid asking them what the examiner asked them. Chances are your conversation with the examiner will be very different and it can only dishearten you to hear that they have been asked something you have not prepared well. It's a no-win situation, so avoid it

During the exam

When you are actually in the exam you can maximise your marks by following these tips I outline below.

Be polite

- Greet the examiner politely in the language of the exam.
- After you have signed beside your name and exam number, and just before you take your seat, look at the examiner, shake their hand and greet them with a translation of something like, 'Hello, nice to meet you.'
- Throughout the exam, stay formal and polite. For example, if you are speaking French, stick to 'vous' (the formal version of 'you') when you address the examiner.
- When you are going, stand up, shake the examiner's hand and leave with a translation of something like, 'Goodbye, thank you.'
- Don't forget to smile!

Don't worry about nerves

All examiners understand that you'll be nervous during your oral exam. So don't worry about it. You will *never* lose marks for nervousness. Accept that you will be nervous and keep it in perspective. In fact, being a little nervous is a good thing as it will aid concentration and pump adrenaline around your body, which will keep you alert and focused. So use the nerves to your advantage.

Don't be afraid

Try not to think of the examiner as the enemy wanting to catch you out. In fact, the examiner wants you to do well and wants to give you the marks. So trust them and allow them to see your real personality. Don't be afraid of them – remember they all had to do oral exams as well, so they understand how you are feeling. And even if you feel you made a fool of yourself in front of your examiner, the chances are that you'll never see them again, so who cares?

Forget the tape

It can be daunting to have a tape recorder in front of you but try to block it out. If you've already practised with a tape, you'll be used to it and can ignore it. Just remember that all students are taped and besides, you'll never have to listen to it.

Look for clarification

At times you might not understand the question asked. The worst thing you can do here is to plough on and answer anyway. What you should do is look for clarification: ask the examiner politely if they can repeat the question. Explain that you don't understand and could he or she please rephrase.

Answer questions fully

Never be content with giving just a 'yes' or 'no' answer. Answer in full sentences and expand out your answers with explanations, examples, information etc. Keep talking until you feel you have given all the information you know about that particular question.

Guide questions

You can somewhat guide the oral exam in the direction you want it to go. If you've prepared material on your favourite music, when you are asked about hobbies you can mention that you like to listen to music, which will probably lead to questions about this.

Stay focused

Focus your attention on the examiner totally. Concentrate on what he or she is saying to you and listen very carefully. If you don't understand a question, don't worry about it. Just ask for clarification and move on. Don't keep harping back in your mind to the question you didn't understand. You can't be expected to understand everything, especially when you are nervous. Give your full attention to the next question and you'll soon forget about that little bump.

Pay attention to verb tense

Listen very carefully to the verb tense the examiner uses. You will probably get questions in the past, present and future tenses, so make sure that you then answer in the appropriate tense.

Admit mistakes

Don't be afraid to admit you made a mistake. If you think you just made an error in a sentence, stop, apologise to the examiner, explain that you made a mistake and correct it. It's better to do this than keep going on, knowing that you made an error.

Take your time

If can be very tempting to rush though the oral exam, just to get it over and done with. And we all tend to speak faster when we are nervous. However, you will make the most of your exam if you take deep breaths, slow down and take your time.

If you need a minute or two to think about your answer, then take the time to do so. The examiner won't rush you and you'll be glad you took the time to gather your thoughts.

Let conversation flow

Remember that the oral is supposed to be a conversation between you and the examiner, not a grilling session. So try to let the conversation flow. While you can somewhat direct the conversation towards areas of interest to you, don't be too obsessed with getting in everything you have learned. Conversations flow off in certain directions sometimes and you should allow this to happen.

If you are particularly uncomfortable with a topic or you feel you have no interest in that area, tell the examiner this politely way and he or she will probably change the direction of the questioning.

Speak clearly

Speak clearly. Look at the examiner and pronounce words clearly. Don't mutter.

Some quick dos and don'ts of oral exams

Do	Don't
Prepare early.	Be sloppy about pronunciation.
Practise lots.	Prepare only vocabulary lists.
Listen to the language.	Be afraid.
Be polite.	Worry too much about nerves.
Speak clearly.	Plough on when you aren't sure about a question.
Prepare topics and set pieces.	Rush yourself.
Ask for clarification.	
Watch verb tenses.	

19 Preparing for aural exams

An aural exam is a test of listening comprehension. You'll be expected to listen to conversations and other spoken items and be able to understand what is being said.

In order to prepare for aural exams you need to listen to as much of the language you're learning as possible.

Preparation strategies

Prepare early

Begin preparation for your aural exam as early as possible. This will give you time to get comfortable with the language. If you leave it too late, you might get panicky and then it becomes more difficult to cram everything in.

This preparation will, of course, also be of great help in preparing for the oral and written exams, so this work serves three purposes and is worth doing well.

Listen carefully in class

Listen very carefully to your teacher as they speak the language. Aim to understand the instructions before they translate them into English.

For more details on listening skills in class see Chapter 7, 'Learning to listen'.

Talk with friends

Meet with other friends who are also learning the language and exchange your daily news. Listen carefully to how they speak. This will open you up to more accents that just your teacher's.

Listen to the language

Listen to as much of the language as you can. The more accents you can listen to, the better. This will give you practice in understanding differing pronunciations of the same words. You can also:

- Watch films in your chosen language.
- Watch TV programmes in this language.

- Get some language CDs and listen to them frequently. Repeat the phrases as you hear them.
- If possible, exchange language time with a native speaker – you'll speak English with them one day, if they speak German with you the next day.

Use past papers

Past exam papers usually come with a CD-ROM for your PC (if you don't have a PC at home, ask for use of the school facilities) and you should use this extensively. The advantage of this is that you can listen to the CD and read the transcript onscreen. Do this regularly and when you've mastered the CD with the transcript, come back to it a few days later and listen without the transcript. Practise answering the questions on the paper that accompanies the CD.

Practise your timing

Practise your timing with the past papers as well. Allow yourself only the same time limit you'll have in the exam.

Practise online

There are many very good websites out there for practising languages. You can find sites that have things like interactive lessons and quizzes and puzzles. Some have spoken word as well. Check with your teacher for any sites he or she would recommend in your particular language or just do an online search for relevant sites.

During the exam

When you are actually in the exam you can maximise your marks by following the tips I outline below.

Read the paper

Take the 5 minutes given at the beginning of the exam to read all the questions on the paper very carefully. Take a highlighter and highlight the main part of the question. This will help you to be clear on what exactly you're being asked to listen out for. Now you'll be able to listen with certain questions in mind, which will help you stay focused.

Stay focused

Focus your attention on the tape totally. Concentrate on what the people are saying and listen very carefully. Listen out for key words that you know and keep the questions in mind.

Listen on first listening

When the first round of the tape is played, don't attempt to answer any questions at this stage. Just listen to the entire tape and get an overall idea of what it is about.

Answer on second listening

The second time around is when you should answer the questions. Fill in as much as you can and don't be overly concerned with spelling – make an attempt. This is not, after all, a spelling test, but a comprehension one, so make a stab at words you're not sure of. If you're stuck on a question, move on when the tape starts again.

Check on third listening

The third listening is for checking back on your answers. Go through each one again, checking that you're happy with what you wrote. If you left any question out first time around, fill it in now. Attempt something. If you're lost, think about the conversation so far, what would you say in this situation? But make sure you fill in something – you might get marks for some of it but you'll never get marks for a blank answer.

(Be careful though in cases like the French aural exam where the news section is only repeated twice.)

Some quick Dos and don'ts of aural exams

Do	Don't
Prepare early.	Leave questions blank.
Practise with past papers.	Be overly concerned with spelling.
Answer on the second listen.	Write answers on the first listen.
Check over your answers on the third listen.	

Section 6

Exam Guides

Leaving Certificate Examination in English

Exam Structure

Higher Level

Paper 1

2 hrs 50 minutes

Allow 10-15 minutes to read the paper

Section 1: Comprehending (100 Marks)

Answer 1 question A on one text and 1 question B on another text

35 minutes per question

Section 2: Composing (100 Marks)

Answer 1 composition (there will be a choice of 7)

Time allowance is about 70 minutes

10 minutes to review your paper

Paper 2

3 hrs 20 minutes

Allow 10 minutes to read the paper

Section 1: Single Text (60 Marks)

Answer 1 of 2 questions

55 minutes

Section 2: Comparative Study (70 marks)

Answer 1 of 2 questions

60 minutes

Section 3: Poetry (70 Marks)

Answer questions on unseen poem and 1 of 4 prescribed poets

Allow 45 minutes for the prescribed poet and 15 minutes for the unseen poem

Allow 10 minutes at the end to review your paper

Ordinary Level

Paper 1

2 hrs 50 minutes

Allow 10–15 minutes to read the paper

Section 1: Comprehending (100 Marks)

Answer 1 question A on one text and 1 question B on another text

Allow 35 minutes per question

Section 2: Composing (100 Marks)

Answer 1 composition (there will be a choice of 7)

Time allowance is about 70 minutes

10 minutes to review your paper

Paper 2

3 hrs 20 minutes

10 minutes to read the paper

Section 1: Single Text (60 Marks)

Answer 1 of 2 questions

55 minutes

Section 2: Comparative Study (70 Marks)

Answer 1 of 2 questions

60 minutes

Section 3: Poetry (70 Marks)

Answer questions on unseen poem and 1 of the prescribed poems

Allow 45 minutes for the prescribed poet and 15 minutes for the unseen poem

Allow 10 minutes at the end to review your paper

Top Ten Things to Remember for the English Exam

1   Read the entire paper before you make any decisions on questions or before you start writing.
2   For Paper 1, know your layouts for Questions B and your categories of language.
3   Know exactly what your single text and comparative texts are. Don't answer on your single text as part of your comparative answer.
4   Keep an eye on the time. Writing can get out of hand sometimes and we can start to waffle. Stay focused on your plan and stick to the time limits.
5   Answer the question that's asked. Avoid summaries and stick to the point of the question.
6   Don't worry unnecessarily about the 'correct' meaning of the unseen poem. Your own interpretation of the poem is what the examiner is looking for, so as long as you can back up your opinion you're OK.
7   When answering on the prescribed poet, aim to include good analysis of *at least* four poems.
8   When answering the comparative question, name your chosen texts at the beginning of the answer and make sure you include lots of links between the texts by using comparing and contrasting language.
9   Plan answers carefully using brainstorms.
10 Proofread your paper closely at the end.

Leaving Certificate Examination in Irish

Higher Level

Total Marks = 600

Oral exam = 150 marks

13-20 minutes

Section 1

Reading of a short prescribed text (30 Marks)

Section 2

Richness of Irish/Vocabulary used (75 Marks)

Linguistic ability (45 Marks)

Answer all questions

Aural exam (100 Marks)

40 minutes

Section A = 30 Marks

Section B = 40 Marks

Section C = 20 Marks

Quality of Irish = 10 Marks

Written Paper

Paper 1 (170 Marks)

2 hrs 50 minutes

Question 1: Composition (100 Marks)

90 minutes

Answer 1 question from A, B, C, D

A = essay

B = story

C = newspaper/magazine article

D = debate/speech

Question 2: Reading comprehensions (35 Marks each)

40 minutes each

2 reading comprehensions with accompanying questions

Paper 2 (180 Marks)

3 hrs 20 minutes

NB Pupils have a choice between prescribed prose and poetry and optional prose and poetry.

Question 1a: Prescribed prose course/1b: Optional prose course (40 Marks)

(a) 25 Marks (30 minutes)

(b) 15 Marks (20 minutes)

Pupils have internal choices in these questions

Question 2: Extra Prose text (40 Marks)

50 minutes

1 question to be answered from A, B, C, D

A = short stories

B = novels

C = autobiographies

D = dramas

Question 3a: Prescribed Poetry/3b: Optional Poetry (35 Marks)

40 minutes

1 of 2 poems to be selected

(a)(i) 12 Marks

(a)(ii) 8 Marks

(b) 15 Marks (no choice here)

Question 3c: Extra Compulsory Poems (35 Marks)

40 minutes

1 of 2 poems to be chosen and accompanying questions answered

(a)(i)   20 Marks

(a)(ii)   6 Marks

(a)(iii)   9 Marks

Question 4: History of Irish (30 Marks)

20 minutes

2 topics to be chosen from sections A, B, C, D, E and F

Ordinary Level

Total Marks = 600

Oral exam (150 Marks)

13-20 minutes

Section 1: Reading of a short prose text (30 Marks)

Section 2: Richness of Irish/Vocabulary used (75 Marks)

Linguistic ability (45 Marks)

Aural exam (120 Marks)

40 minutes

Section A = 42 Marks

Section B = 51 Marks

Section C = 27 Marks

Written exam

Paper 1 (220 marks)

2 hrs 20 minutes

Question 1: Composition (60 Marks X 2) (45 minutes to be spent at each)

2 questions to be answered from either A, B, C or D

A = short written passage

B = continuation of a given opening story

C = letter

D = conversation

Question 2: Reading Comprehensions (50 Marks X 2) (25 minutes each)

2 reading comprehensions with 5 questions accompanying each one

Paper 2 (110 Marks)

2 hrs 20 minutes

NB Pupils have a choice between Sections A and Sections B

<u>Section A:</u> Prescribed course = 55 Marks (70 minutes)

<u>Section B:</u> Optional course = 55 Marks (70 minutes)

<u>Section A:</u> Prescribed Course

Question 1 – Prose (5 stories to be covered)

(a)(i) 25 Marks

(ii) 10 Marks

Question 1 – Prose

(b) 20 Marks

Pupils have internal choices within these questions

Question 2 – Poetry (5 poems to be covered)

(a)(i) 25 Marks

(ii) 10 Marks

Question 2 – Poetry

(b) 20 Marks

<u>Section B:</u> Optional Course

Question 1 – Prose

(a)(i) 25 Marks

(ii) 10 Marks

Question 1 – Prose

(b) 20 Marks

Question 2 – Poetry

(a)(i) 35 Marks

Question 2 – Poetry

(b) 20 Marks

Foundation Level

Total Marks = 600

Oral exam (150 Marks)

4 blocks of topics to be covered @ 30 Marks per block

Overall effort/attempt and grammar = 30 Marks

Aural exam (180 Marks)

40 minutes

12 questions with some subdivided into Parts (a) and (b)

Written Paper (270 Marks)

2 hrs 50 minutes

Reading Section = 150 Marks

80 minutes

Question 1: Matching (40 Marks)

Question 2: 5 questions to be answered from 2 out of 3 passages (25 Marks x 2)

Question 3: 5 questions to be answered from 2 out of 3 passages (30 Marks x 2)

Writing Section (120 Marks)

90 minutes

Question 4: Write a notice or an invitation/reply using a sequence of pictures (30 Marks)

Question 5: Write a letter (using a pictorial sequence) or fill in an application form (40 Marks)

Question 6: Write an account from a pictorial sequence or write an account about an event from a sequence of pictures given (50 Marks)

Timing:

(1) Matching @ 40 Marks = 10 minutes

(2) 2 Reading comprehensions @ 25 Marks each = 15 minutes X 2

(3) 2 Reading comprehensions @ 30 Marks each = 20 minutes each

(4) Writing of a 'notice' or an 'invitation/reply' @ 30 Marks = 25 minutes

(5) Letter of an application form to be filled in @ 40 Marks = 30 minutes

(6) A written account of a picture sequence @ 50 Marks = 35 minutes

Top Ten Things to Remember for the Irish Exam

1 Begin preparations for the *oral exam* early and prepare well.

2 Watch Teilifís na Gaeilge and tune into Raidio na Life or Raidio na Gaeltachta. You'll become more familiar with different dialects and this in turn will benefit your aural and oral papers.

3 Attempt all questions in the *aural exam*. Try to write down the words you hear even if you're unsure of the spelling – this isn't a spelling test but a comprehending one, so don't be overly concerned with spelling.

4 For the *written exam*, know which poetry and prose course you're studying and answering questions on – the prescribed course or the optional one.

5 Read and choose questions very carefully.

6 Complete the reading comprehensions first and this will leave you time to concentrate on the writing tasks.

7 Be careful to read the titles of stories/essay very carefully and be sure you understand them.

8 When writing stories, letters, conversations etc. in Paper 1 at Ordinary Level, keep sentences short and accurate. Know 20 key phrases that you can use in almost any context. This will improve the 'richness' of your Gaeilge and earn more marks.

9 At Higher Level, try to put the answers to the reading comprehensions in your own words. Avoid copying chunks of the passages, as you'll lose marks for this.

10 Attempt all the questions you should at any level. You can't get marks for a blank space but you might get marks for the attempt.

Leaving Certificate Examination in Mathematics

Exam Structure

Higher Level

Paper 1 (300 Marks. All questions 50 Marks each)

2 hrs 30 minutes

Allow 10 minutes to read the paper

8 Questions, answer 6

Each question should take about 20 minutes

Allow 10 minutes to review your paper

Paper 2 (300 Marks. All questions 50 Marks each)

2 hrs 30 minutes

Allow 10 minutes to read the paper

Section A: 7 Questions, answer 5

Section B: 4 Questions, answer 1

Each question should take about 20 minutes

Allow 10 minutes to review your paper

Ordinary Level

Paper 1 (300 Marks. All questions 50 Marks each)

2 hrs 30 minutes

Allow 10 minutes to read the paper

8 Questions, answer 6

Each question should take about 20 minutes

Allow 10 minutes to review your paper

Paper 2 (300 Marks. All questions 50 Marks each)

2 hrs 30 minutes

Allow 10 minutes to read the paper

<u>Section A:</u> 7 Questions, answer 5

<u>Section B:</u> 4 Questions, answer 1

Each question should take about 20 minutes

Allow 10 minutes to review your paper

Foundation Level

Paper 1 (300 Marks. All questions 50 Marks each)

2 hrs 30 minutes

Allow 10 minutes to read the paper

7 Questions, answer Q1 and four others

Each question should take about 20 minutes

Allow 10 minutes to review your paper

Paper 2 (300 Marks. All questions 50 Marks each)

2 hrs 30 minutes

Allow 10 minutes to read the paper

8 Questions, answer 6

Each question should take about 20 minutes

Allow 10 minutes to review your paper

Top Ten Things to Remember for the Mathematics Exam

1   Know the layout of the papers very well; know where various topics arise.

2   Identify your areas of strength and weakness long before the exam.

3   Concentrate on your strengths to ensure maximum marks in these questions.

4   Know algebra really well, as it can come up on many different questions.

5   Do your best question first.

6   Attempt all parts of questions. Part (a) is straight forward; Part (b) a little harder; and Part (c) harder still. Don't leave out a part of a question; try it at least.

7   Mistakes with signs cost 3 marks but may actually make the question impossible to finish, so make sure your know the rules.

8   If you get finished before the time, don't leave. Check back carefully over all your answers and if you still have time, try another question; you'll be marked out of the best ones.

9   Know your formulae and where to access them in the exam. (At Foundation Level, all required formulae are provided.)

10 Have all the equipment you need for the exam. Not having a compass, for example, can be distracting and disruptive and will increase stress levels and lower concentration. So just have everything with you.

Leaving Certificate Examination in History

Exam Structure

Candidates will answer four questions, one on each of the four topics studied. All four questions will be of equal value.

The first question on the paper will be document based.

Documents-based Topic, Allocation of Marks, Ordinary Level:

Comprehension: 40

Comparison: 20

Criticism: 20

Contextualisation: 20

Documents-based Topic, Allocation of Marks, Higher Level:

Comprehension: 20

Comparison: 20

Criticism: 20

Contextualisation: 40

Sections 2 and 3 of the Higher Level paper will ask candidates to respond to an historical question. Four questions will be asked on each topic, with candidates answering one of these on their chosen topics.

Timing:

Document-Based Topic: 45 minutes

General Questions: each 35 minutes

Top Ten Things to Remember for the History Exam

1   Read the question carefully, underlining keywords. The question will be about a specific event, person or era, so you must decide what information is being asked for.

2   Words such as discuss, analyse, evaluate, explain... will not appear in the question. These words invite you to write down everything you know, you must focus your answer on the person, event or era that the question mentions.

3   Always have a clear structure for your essay answers: beginning, middle and end. Remember, history is about cause and effect, so structure your answers chronologically, what caused the event, what happened during the event and what consequences the event had.

4   Know the case studies inside out! They will feature heavily in the questions.

5   Always write in short, neat paragraphs. Make one point well per paragraph, even if it only takes a few lines. Your answers will be marked one paragraph at a time.

6   When revising, create a glossary of key words for each topic. Structure your answers around these words. They will help you remember the key events and personalities.

7   Always write in sequence with events, begin at the beginning, end at the end.

8   Don't be afraid to give your interpretation of events, display your analytical skill.

9   Bullet points are OK in the following situations only:
   • listing advantages or disadvantages
   • listing demands or needs
   • listing the goals of an organisation or an individual
   • listing successes or failures.

10 Concentrate on what you do know; you can't do anything about what you don't.

Leaving Certificate Examination in Geography

Exam Structure

Higher Level

2 hrs 50 minutes.

There are 400 Marks for the exam and 100 for the Field Work Booklet. Total 500 Marks.

Part 1

12 short answer questions, answer 10

10 x 8 = 80 Marks

Part 2

Structured and Essay Questions.

<u>Section 1:</u>

Students must do any one from the questions 1-3

All questions will have three parts.

80 Marks.

Students must do any one from the three questions 4-6

All questions will have three parts.

80 Marks.

<u>Section 2:</u>

Electives.

Q7-9 and 10-13.

There are three questions on each of the two

Electives

Students must do one question from the one elective course they have studied.

80 Marks.

There will be three parts to every question.

Section 3:

Options.

Students must answer one essay-type question on the option they have studied.

There are three questions on each option.

80 Marks

Timing:

Each question is worth 80 Marks, there are 5 questions to do so students should spend 35 minutes on each with 15 minutes left over for review.

Ordinary Level

Part 1

12 short answer questions, answer 10

10 x 10 = 100 Marks

Part 2

Section 1:

Students must do any one from the questions 1-3

All questions will have three parts.

100 Marks.

Students must do any one from the three questions from 4-6

All questions will have three parts.

100 Marks.

Section 2:

Electives. Questions 7-9 and 10-13.

There are three questions on each of the two electives.

Students must do one question from the one elective course they have studied

100 Marks.

There will be three parts to every question.

Timing:

Each question is worth 80 Marks, there are 5 questions to do so students should spend 35 minutes on each with 15 minutes left over for review.

Top Ten Things to Remember for the Geography Exam

1 Practise drawing sketch maps from aerial photos and maps. Don't forget to include a frame, a key and to use colouring pencils.

2 Study the processes of erosion and deposition and link them to the landscape features formed by them. Include a diagram and definition with your description of each feature as well as two examples.

3 Make sure you can recognise on maps, photos and from diagrams Fluvial, Glacial <u>and</u> Marine features.

4 Case studies are vital in the exams, especially for things like earthquakes, Volcanic Eruptions, Tsunami but also for areas like Dam Building, Quarrying, Canalisation etc. Use some facts and figures with your case study to back up your answers and show the examiner you have an awareness of Geographical phenomenon.

5 Be able to compare a core and peripheral area in Ireland by being able to write a short comparative paragraph on each of the five processes you have studied - Physical, Primary, Secondary, Tertiary and Human. Be able to explain why one is peripheral and the other a core using each of these processes.

6 Prepare bullet points on each of your European regions and you Sub Continental region using these same five processes as headings; <u>but</u> do not use bullet points in the exams.

7 Answers are marked on SRPs – Significant Relevant Points. So don't waffle and have plenty of short sentences so the examiner can see your points.

8 Each elective is divided into clear sections – consult your textbook. Make sure you treat each equally. For the Economic Elective, practise interpreting graphs and tables and for the Human Elective, practise map and photo reading skills.

9 For the Option you will have to write an essay. Make sure you use plenty of paragraphs, each with a separate idea or development. Refer to the question. In terms of study, you need to make bullet point notes on each section of the option and practise essays dealing with every facet of the option.

10 Practise your timing at home and in school. You know how long you have in the exams so try to get used to managing your time.

Leaving Certificate Examination in French

Exam Structure

Higher Level

Written Exam (200 Marks)

2 hrs 30 minutes

10 minutes to read the paper

2 Sections

<u>Section 1:</u> Reading Comprehension (120 Marks)

2 questions (60 Marks each)

Answer all parts of both questions

35 minutes each

<u>Section 2:</u>

Written Assignments (100 Marks)

Question 1 = 40 Marks

Other questions = 30 Marks

Answer question 1 based on text 1 or 2, and 2 remaining questions

Question 1, 30 minutes; 20 minutes each for other 2 questions

Aural exam (80 Marks)

5 Sections

Answer all questions

40 minutes

Oral exam (100 Marks)

Informal Conversation; no definite amount of questions

Answer all questions

Approx. 15 minutes

Ordinary Level

Written exam (200 Marks)

2 hrs 30 minutes

10 minutes to read the paper

2 sections

<u>Section 1:</u> Reading Comprehension (160 Marks)

4 questions (40 Marks each)

Answer all four texts, all questions

25 minutes each

<u>Section 2:</u> Written Assignments (60 Marks)

3 questions, 30 Marks each

Answer 2 questions out of A, B or C

20 minutes each

Aural exam (100 Marks)

5 sections

Answer all questions

40 minutes

Oral exam (80 Marks)

Informal Conversation; no definite amount of questions

Answer all questions

Approx. 15 minutes

Top Ten Things to Remember for the French Exam

1   Prepare for the <u>oral exam</u> early and well. Have your topics covered well and prepare and bring in a French document, a photo or project with you. This preparation is also useful for the aural and written exams.

2   Try to relax and let conversation flow in the oral. Smile and be polite.

3   In the <u>aural exam</u>, take the time given at the beginning of the exam to read over the paper carefully. Highlight key words in the questions.

4   Don't answer any questions when you listen to the tape the first time. Write answers on the second listening and check over them on the third. Be careful with the news section though (Section 5), as you'll only hear each item **twice**.

5   In the <u>written exam</u>, don't worry if you can't understand the comprehension passages on first reading. Take your time and read them a few times and you'll understand more as you read.

6   Read questions very carefully and answer the question asked. Avoid transcribing or translating large chunks of passages. Stick to shorter quotes and your own words. Extraneous information that is not directly answering the question will be penalised, so avoid this at all costs.

7   Familiarise yourself with common instructions like 'Redigez' (redraft), 'Citez' (quote).

8   Be very careful to distinguish when you need to answer in French and when you need to answer in English.

9   Watch your grammar in all areas of the exam.

10 In all areas of the exam match the tenses of verbs. Pay close attention to the verb tense in the question and match it in your answer. In the oral when asked a question, the examiner will ask in the –'ez' form of the verb, so be careful to not mimic this form of the verb in your answer. For example you might be asked, 'Qu'est-ce-que vous preferez, comme sport?' and you need to answer with the 'Je prefere' form of the verb, not with 'Je preferez'.

Leaving Certificate Examination in German

Exam Structure

Higher Level

Written Exam (220 Marks)

2 hrs 30 minutes

Text 1: Reading Comprehension – Literary Extract (60 Marks)

Answer all 4 questions

Text 1: Applied Grammar (25 Marks)

Answer both questions

Text II: Reading Comprehension (60 Marks)

Answer all 4 questions

Text II: Related Written Expression (25 Marks)

Answer A or B

Written Production (50 Marks)

Answer A or B

Aural exam (80 Marks)

Answer all questions

40 minutes

Oral exam (100 Marks)

Informal Conversation; no definite amount of questions

Answer all questions

Approx. 15 minutes.

Ordinary Level
Written Exam (220 Marks)

2 hrs 30 minutes

Text 1: Reading Comprehension – Literary Extract (60 Marks)

Answer all 4 questions

Text 1: Applied Grammar (15 Marks)

Answer both questions

Text II: Reading Comprehension – Non-literary text (60 Marks)

Answer all questions

Text II: Related Written Expression (15 Marks)

Answer A or B

Text III: Reading Comprehension – Non-literary text (40 Marks)

Answer all questions

Written Production (30 Marks)

Answer A or B

Aural exam (80 Marks)

Answer all questions.

40 minutes

Oral exam (100 Marks)

Informal Conversation; no definite amount of questions

Answer all questions

Approx. 15 minutes

Top Ten Things to Remember for the German Exam

1 Prepare for the <u>oral exam</u> early and well. Have your topics covered well and prepare your set piece well. This preparation is also useful for the aural and written exams.

2 Try to relax and let conversation flow in the oral. Smile and be polite.

3 In the <u>aural exam</u>, take the time given at the beginning of the exam to read over the paper carefully. Highlight key words in the questions.

4 Don't answer any questions when you listen to the tape the first time. Write answers on the second listening and check over them on the third.

5 In the <u>written exam</u>, don't worry if you can't understand the comprehension passages on first reading. Take your time and read them a few times and you'll understand more as you read.

6 Read questions very carefully and answer the question asked. Avoid transcribing or translating large chunks of passages. Stick to shorter quotes and your own words. Extraneous information that is not directly answering the question will be penalised, so avoid this at all costs.

7 Familiarise yourself with common instructions that you'll come across on the paper.

8 Be very careful to distinguish when you need to answer in German and when you need to answer in English.

9 Watch your grammar in all areas of the exam.

10 In all areas of the exam match the tenses of verbs. Pay close attention to the verb tense in the question and match it in your answer.

Leaving Certificate Examination in Biology

Exam Structure

Higher and Ordinary Level

<u>Section A:</u> Short questions (100 Marks)

30 minutes (6 mins per question)

6 questions, answer 5

Unit 1: 2 questions

Unit 2: 2 questions

Unit 3: 2 questions

Each question carries 20 Marks

<u>Section B:</u> Lab questions (60 Marks)

20 minutes (10 minutes per question)

3 questions, answer 2

Questions taken from list of 22 experiments

Each question carries 30 marks

<u>Section C:</u> Long questions (40 Marks)

20 minutes (30 minutes per question)

6 questions, answer 4

Unit 1: 1 question

Unit 2: 2 questions

Unit 3: 3 questions

Each question carries 60 marks

Top Ten Things to Remember for the Biology Exam

1   Know the layout of the exam: how many sections there are and how many questions have to be answered.

2   Be aware of the time you have to answer 7 (5 & 2) short questions and 4 long questions in 3 hours.

3   Section A short questions: practise by answering questions from past exam papers.

4   Section B Mandatory lab experiments are worth 15% of your total marks. Make sure you are familiar with the 22 experiments, what materials and method used and why. Practise by answering questions from past exam papers.

5   Prepare long questions from Section C, by using past papers.

6   There are some topics that cannot be ignored:
   • food tests and types
   • ecology
   • genetics
   • photosynthesis and respiration
   • plant biology.

7   Make sure you know what topics can be linked e.g. (food, enzymes, nutrition, excretion), (Nervous system and Endocrine system) etc.

8   Be aware of topical issues as they can appear in exam questions, the papers are usually set in the December of the previous year, e.g. global warming, natural disasters, DNA (50th anniversary of Crick Watson was in 2003 and DNA featured heavily in the Genetics question).

9   Diagrams are very important in Biology you must know how to draw and label them.

10   It can be very helpful to try and relate the topics in Biology to your real life.

Leaving Certificate Examination in Chemistry

Exam Structure

Higher and Ordinary Level

Section A: is based on the 28 mandatory experiments

You must answer at least 2 out of 3 questions

Section B: 8 questions covering the entire course

You must answer 5 or 6, depending on how many you answered in Section A

Total no. of questions = 8 from both sections

Time = 3 hours

Approx. 20 minutes per question + 20 minutes extra time (to read paper at the start and then read over answers at end)

Top Ten Things to Remember for the Chemistry Exam

1 **Know your experiments**. In Section A you are asked 3 questions and you must answer at least 2. There are 28 experiments on the course and they can also appear as part of other questions in Section B.
2 When revising Section A, revise past questions from solutions. The last parts of these questions are calculations so make sure you have practised working them out.
3 Know the layout of the exam: how many sections there are and how many questions have to be answered. You must answer 8 questions out of 11.
4 Watch your timing. Give yourself 20 minutes per question. This leaves 20 minutes for time to read the paper at beginning and the end of the exam.
5 Revise past exam papers. Course changed in 2002 so use papers for past 4 years. When revising each topic, revise past questions from solutions.
6 Question 11 options topics are relatively easy and are very predictable. Make sure you know these.
7 Use flash cards for learning formulae (Boyles Law, Charles law, etc.) and shapes of organic (alkanes, alkenes, alkynes) and inorganic compounds.
8 Chemistry can be a difficult subject but if you put the work in early on it will pay off. Work from day one and don't leave everything until the last minute.
9 Know your basics. Start at the periodic table, methods of bonding, shapes of compounds. All of the harder topics require you to have a good understanding of these basic principles
10 Read questions carefully and answer all parts of all questions. Never leave a blank space where there should be an answer.

Leaving Certificate Examination in Physics

Exam Structure

Higher Level

<u>Section A:</u> Practical/Lab Work Questions (120 Marks: 30% of total)

51 minutes: 17 minutes per question

4 questions, answer 3

Questions taken from list of 24 experiments (There are <u>four</u> conducting media for investigation of variation of Current with PD)

Each question carries 40 Marks

<u>Section B:</u> Long questions (280 Marks: 70% of total)

110 minutes (22 minutes per question)

8 questions, answer 5

One question: 10 parts – each carries 7 Marks – Answer any 8

One Question: 2 Options – Answer 1 (*Particle Physics* or *Applied Electricity*)

One question: 4 parts (a,b,c,d) – Each carries 28 Marks – Answer any 2

Five other questions carry 56 Marks each – all parts to be answered

Each question carries 56 Marks

Ordinary Level

<u>Section A:</u> Practical/Lab Work Questions (120 Marks: 30% of total)

51 minutes (17 minutes per question)

4 questions, answer 3

Questions taken from list of 24 experiments (There are <u>four</u> conducting media for investigation of variation of Current with PD)

Each question carries 40 Marks

<u>Section B:</u> Long questions (280 Marks: 70% of total)

110 minutes (22 minutes per question)

8 questions, answer 5

One question: 10 parts – each carries 7 Marks – Answer any 8

One question: 4 parts (a,b,c,d) – Each carries 28 Marks – Answer any 2

Six other questions carry 56 Marks each – all parts to be answered

Each question carries 56 Marks

Top Ten Things to Remember for the Physics Exam

1 Familiarise yourself with the structure and layout of the paper – use past papers as a guideline for this.

2 Definitions of terms and units: This is crucial to all aspects of the paper. Questions also carry an STS component (Science, Technology, Society) so it is important to familiarise yourself with practical applications of Physics principles.

3 Make sure you know how to use data collected during the experimental procedures for the mandatory experiments on Section A. Most marks in this section are allocated to this.

4 Practise answering questions on practicals that can be asked on Section B (Apparatus, procedure, observations/data, conclusion). Always draw a diagram to illustrate your answer where possible. Remember that it is essential to keep diagrams clear and well labelled.

5 Remember that Question 11 (Option) carries the same marks as any other question but only one option may be answered.

6 The 'problem' component of each question is usually linked to the part that precedes it, so whatever theory/definition/formula required will usually be based on the previous part of the question. Make sure to write the correct unit in each case.

7 When preparing any topic, look at past papers to see how the topic is examined and try to cover the variety of approaches to questions on the topic.

8 Marks are allocated for the most part in blocks of 3 Marks, so when answering any question, keep answers to the point and think of a 12-Mark part as 4 blocks of 3 Marks each.

9 The fundamental principles of Mechanics Section are essential to understanding many of the other topics on the course, so it is important to invest the effort required in understanding these principles.

10 The time available is adequate to answer all that is required, but you must manage your time and stick to your plan. Give yourself time 51 minutes at Section A (17 minutes per question) and 110 minutes at Section B (22 minutes per question) This leaves 19 minutes to be divided for reading the paper at beginning and to read over your script at the end.

Leaving Certificate Examination in Home Economics

Exam Structure

2 hrs 30 minutes

Section A

30 minutes

12 questions, answer 10 questions

Each question carries equal Marks

Section B

30 minutes per question

5 questions, answer question 1 and any 2 other questions. Question 1 is worth 80 Marks

Questions 2, 3, 4 and 5 are worth 50 Marks each

Section C

30 minutes per question

3 questions, answer 1 elective question to include Part (a), and either Part (b) or Part (c)

Electives 1 and 3 are worth 80 Marks and Elective 2 is worth 4 Marks

Elective 1 is home design and management. Elective 2 is textiles fashion and design and Elective 3 is social studies

Only those candidates who have submitted a textiles fashion and design project should attempt Elective 2

Structure of course and allocation of marks

Marks in the leaving certificate home economic exam are allocated as follows:

Food studies: 45%

Resource management and consumer studies: 25%

Social studies: 10%

The elective area:

Home design and management: 20%

Textiles fashion and design: 20%

Social studies: 20%

Top Ten Things to Remember for the Home Economics Exam

1 Know your chosen elective area well.
2 Answer only on the elective area you have studied.
3 Only answer on the textile question if you have completed a textile project.
4 Know the food groups really well.
5 Know the nutrients section well.
6 Practise all short questions with past papers.
7 Organise revision so there is a clear connection between each chapter and section of the course. Observe how topics relate to exam questions to prevent you becoming bogged down in insufficient details.
8 In the exam read the question carefully: the examiner will be looking for specific information on a topic and you should not be tempted to put down a pre-learned question, which does not answer the question asked.
9 Take time to familiarise yourself with the paper by reading it before you begin. This will prevent you missing a vital section of a question and give you time to settle your nerves before you begin.
10 Practise drawing diagrams, remember to place a heading and label each part clearly. Refer to your diagram often when answering the question.

Leaving Certificate Examination in Business Studies

Exam Structure

Higher Level

3 hrs

3 sections

Section 1: Short questions (80 Marks)

32 minutes answering the short questions; i.e. 4 minutes per question

10 short questions, answer any 8 of these

80 Marks going for the short questions, therefore 10 Marks per question

Section 2: Applied Business (80 Marks)

Allow approximately 32 minutes to answer

Answer all 3 questions

The Applied Business question is COMPULSORY. You must do this question

Section 3: Long questions (240 Marks)

Approx. 22 minutes for each question

Answer 4 questions in Section 3

1 question from Part 1

2 questions from Part 2

1 other question from either Part 1 or Part 2

All questions carry equal marks (60 Marks each)

Ordinary Level

2 hrs 30 minutes

2 sections

Section 1: Short questions (100 Marks)

Allow 40-45 minutes for this section

15 questions, answer 10

Section 2: Long questions (300 Marks)

Approx. 22 minutes for each question

8 questions, answer 4 (75 Marks each)

Top Ten things to remember for the Business Studies Exam

1   Always pay close attention to the marking scheme in the exam. Look at how many marks are going for a question and divide this number by 5 to see how many points the examiner requires you to give in your answer. For example, if the question is worth 30 Marks the examiner is looking for 6 relevant points for that question. If the question is worth 10 Marks the examiner is looking for 2 relevant points. (Always include examples where possible).

2   When answering the Short questions always give **two** relevant points in your answer, except where you are specifically asked to give more than two points.

3   When answering the Long questions on Section 3 of the exam paper always structure your answers in the following way to obtain maximum marks:
   • Name the point you are making.
   • Explain the point you are making.
   • Give an example that illustrates the point you're making.

4   At Higher Level, in the Applied Business question you should structure your answer as follows:
   • Name your point.
   • Explain your point.
   • Quote from the text.
   It is very important to quote from the text in the Applied Business question. The examiner wants you to show that you can apply your knowledge of business to the scenario in the text. Hence, the name 'Applied Business' question. Always remember that your quotes must be relevant to the question asked.

5   Avoid repetition. There is no point in giving the same point in a few different ways. This will only irritate the examiner and it will not earn you any more points.

6   Use good business English in your answers. Try to use business terms in your answers. For example, instead of saying a quarrel in work you could say an 'Industrial Relations Dispute'. Instead of saying a middleman who tries to solve disputes, you would say an 'arbitrator' or a 'conciliator' etc.

7   When you're asked to explain the effects/impacts of something you must give the positive *and* the negative effects. Therefore, you must mention the good and bad effects.

8   Always try to apply your knowledge of business to the real world. Give examples from real-life companies/products/situations, etc. This will persuade the examiner that you really do know your subject.

9 Always structure your answers clearly. Give a short introduction in the long questions. Then number the points you're giving. Next give a short conclusion to your answer. (You could perhaps name the points you are making in red pen and put each point in a different paragraph to make it easier for the examiner to correct!)

10 In the **Ratio question** always remember to comment on the ratios after you have done your calculations. You should give **three** comments for each ratio you calculate. The examiner wants to see that you know what the figures actually mean.

Feel good factor comes after you complete work

Plan.

Execute each piece of work carefully – you will
file it after you get it back,
Go back to the teacher – if not good enough mark.

Plan. homework pg 36 – v. important.

marymcell@gmail.com

1940/50

Korea

Overview sl K the period
write pt the period
website pt the period